The World of the Greeks

The World of the Greeks

Texts by **Victor Duruy**

Translated by Joël Rosenthal

Minerva

Contents

Photos : Alinari/Giraudon : 7 - 11b - 66 - 67a - 92a — Alinari/Viollet : 6a - 12 - 31a - 46 - 49a - 50 - 52 - 55 - 57 - 61b - 74 - 82 - 85a - 87b - 102 - 117 - 121 - 132a - 137 - 151 — Anderson/Viollet : 30b - 38 - 76b - 77b - 83a - 94a - 97 - 100 - 101a - 116 - 132c - 146 - 153 — Archiv 8 - 13a - 32b - 93 - 122a, b — Atlas/Boyer : 26a — Giraudon : 9 - 10 - 13b - 20 - 22a, b - 23 - 34 - 35 - 53 - 62 - 68 - 71 - 72 - 75a, b - 76a - 77a - 85b - 86a, b, c, - 94b - 101b, c - 105 - 109 - 113a - 123a - 132b - 141a - 142 - 145 - 148 - 149 — Harlingue : 43 - 48 — Hétier/Atlas : 89, 107 — San/Viollet : 21 - 60 - 147 — Viollet : 2 - 5 - 6b - 11a - 14a, b - 15 - 16 - 17 - 18 - 19a, b, c - 24a, b - 26b - 29 - 32a, c - 36 - 37 - 40b, c - 44 - 45a, b - 47 - 49b - 51a, b - 54 - 56, 58a, b - 59 - 61a - 64 - 65 - 67b - 78 - 79 - 80 - 81 - 83b, c, d - 84a, b - 87a - 88 - 90 - 91a, b - 92b - 98 - 99 - 103 - 104 - 108 - 110 - 111 - 112 - 113b - 114a, b - 115a - 118 - 120 - 125 - 126 - 127a, b - 129a, b - 130a, b - 131- 134 - 135a, b - 138 - 139 - 141b - 143 - 144 - 150 - 152 - 154 - 155 - 156 — Walmann : 30a - 31b - 33 - 39a - 40a - 115b - 119a, b - 123b - 124 - 136.

End pages: Athens, the Temple of Zeus.
Frontispiece: Columns of the Temple of Zeus, Athens.

A Greek landscape: the Nemean plain. It was here, according to legend, that Hercules killed the lion.

1 - The Land of the Hellenes

"What do you mean by Greece?" Philip of Macedon ironically asked the Aetolians when they reproached him for being a barbarian king. "Where are its boundaries? And are most of you Greek?"

This name had the same sort of history as that of Italy: both traveled from one end to the other of a peninsula which later took the name to designate its entirety. Dodona, a small canton of Epirus, first used the name; but the name spread, little by little, reaching Thessaly, the region south of Thermopylae, and the Peloponnesus. It later still included Epirus, Illyria as far as Epidamnus, and finally Macedonia. Another curious point is that the name *Greece* was unknown in Greece: it was called *Hellas,* the land of the Hellenes, and we do not know what reasoning was behind the choice of the word *Graecia* in the Roman language.

Taken on the whole, Greece was not fertile enough to nourish an idle population, nor was it so poor as to need to compel its inhabitants to exert all energy in searching for means of subsistence. The diversity of its land of plains and mountains, and of its climate, varying from the snows of the Pindus to the almost Asiatic cultivation of the Peloponnesus, imposed upon these people a variety of works which develops skills and creates a body of ideas growing out of knowledge, that is, a civilization. More than for any other people, the Greeks were forced by their land to be both shepherds and farmers, but above all, merchants.

And like their land, the Greeks had a

5

"Broad-chested Greeks..."

its fertile countrysides of Marathon and Eleusis producing a ratio of sixty to one, with its olive trees and perfumed honey of Hymettus, its Pentelic marble and Mount Laurium mines, its air so clear that one could supposedly see from Cape Sunium Minerva's aigrette and spear on the Acropolis; and in addition to this, there is the sea bounding the region on three sides. When the Athenians climbed to the top of the Parthenon, they could see these numerous islands scattered around them among the sea's waves, as if inviting them to make them their realm, or to readily lead them, by "wet routes", to the shores of Thrace, Asia and Egypt. Each morning the north wind rose to gently carry their ships to the Cyclades; each night the opposing wind brought them back to port under a star-lighted sky. "Sweet and soft is our air,", said an Athenian poet, "winter is without harshness for us, and never are we harmed by the rays of Phoebus."

severe nature, making them active and muscular. Their broad chests were those of the deep-breathing men of the mountains; although they were not especially tall, they were powerful in physical combat, resistant to fatigue, and fast on their legs; after assuring their own independence, these military qualities made them rulers of Asia. Nature had graced them with beautiful faces; life in the open air and continual exercise developed the elegant proportions of their bodies, and artists had only to look around them for models.

And one must add to this variegated land, where no two valleys are alike, that there was an equal variety of customs and institutions, producing a universal restlessness, in market-places as in minds, and everywhere a sense of effort and struggle. No other people have endured quite like the Greeks.

The faults and advantages of the land, plus its coastline, where earth and sea meet harmoniously, are perfectly summarized in one of Greece's regions: this is Attica, with

"The fertile lands of Marathon and Eleusis..." A sheaf of wheat from a bas-relief in Eleusis.

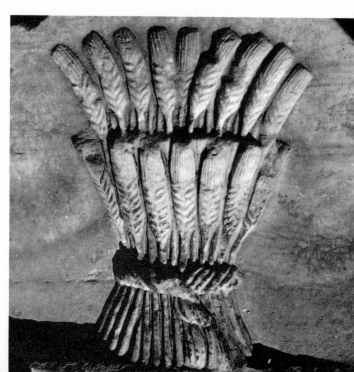

2 - Legendary times

However far back we go into its history, we always find in Greece the custom of assemblies and public disussion. The need to convince before commanding sharpened the spirit of these people; thus all its faculties were kept alive and going, preparing for a most brilliant flight. Free in its political constitution, it was even more so in its religious organization: no priests, or rather, no separate clerical order, and no holy book, such as the Bible or the Vedas, that is, no body of holy doctrine, two important basic facts in the history of the Hellenes' intellectual development.

Just as the head of the family is the priest of the home, so the king is the city's first pontiff: "You watch over the family of this land" the daughters of Danaus say to the king of Argos. It is he, in fact, who sacrifices the victim for his people, without believing himself invested with a holy spirit; when he makes a sacrifice in the name of his city, he is carrying out a public duty.

But superstition is one of man's most natural instincts, and worship has never yet been limited to an act of adoration or gratitude toward the sovereign Being. All peoples have wanted to seize the secrets that the future will always hold, and all have had witches, magicians, or like the Greeks, soothsayers who interpreted heavenly signs, hallucinated individuals who saw the invisible world, and convulsionists, like Pythia of Delphi, who felt god acting and expressing his will within themselves. The Greeks believed that these prophets were in direct contact with the divinity and consulted them with complete confidence. Thus the temple of Dodona had its sacred doves as well as its ancient oaks, which the wind made speak by passing through their foliage; three priestesses, the Peleiads, interpreted these obscure sounds. The oracles of Apollo at Delphi, received by Pythia, were translated

"The custom of assemblies and public discussion..." At Delphi, a public meeting place.

through her priests; and Orpheus accompanied the Argonauts not only to charm their long trip with his songs, but to explain heavenly signs as well.

During Greece's heroic ages, customs were simple because of limited means, but combined with a liberty that was unknown in the Orient. At this time the servile class barely exists, if at all; those who have been taken in war or purchased are less slaves than servants. The dying Alcestis holds out his hand to his slaves for the last farewell. Emmaeus hoped that Ulysses, coming back to Ithaca, would grant him a house, a piece of land and a wife, and upon meeting his master's son would kiss his forehead and eyes; but already the old shepherd says what all Greece, even its philosophers, will say: "The gods take away half of man's qualities the day they make him a slave."

The slaves' position is an easy one, that of women is honored. Here, domestic society, the family, is better established than in the oriental peoples, excepting the Jews, an assurance that political society will also be better established in fairness and liberty. Polygamy is forbidden, but not concubinage. If the Greek woman was still purchased, she was nevertheless no longer condemned to the obscurity and solitude of the harem; she lived openly, at least in earlier times; later her existence would seem more harsh: in Athens she would be locked in the gynaeceum or women's quarters, and would remain in an inferior legal position to her husband. Excluded from her husband's inheritance, her sons' ward, she would remain a minority. The links of the chain that formerly bound her in servitude were not all broken. And yet there would be improvement for her, since the dowry which would become her property would assure her future. Laërtes buys Eurycleia, "But," says Homer, "though she was very young, he did not make her his companion, fearing his wife." Since the hero does not disdain manual labor, the woman is thus left with the domestic chores. Even the king's daughters draw water from the fountains, as do the beautiful Nausicaa, and Polyxena, Priam's daughter. Andromache feeds Hector's horses; Helen works at marvelous embroideries; and Penelope can calm the suitors' patience only by showing them the last garment she is preparing for the old Laërtes, this fabric which she weaves during the day and undoes at night: "What would the women of Greece say if I left this hero without a shroud when the Fates carry him to his death?"

However, in this age when strength and

"Woman's position is an honored one..." *Right: this ancient statue comes from Crete.*

daring are honored, infidelity is not an unpardonable crime. The adulterer is never very severely punished. The guilty wife is merely marked down for an infamous action; she can no longer wear certain ornaments or attend public sacrifices. If she does not obey these rules, she may then have her other ornaments and clothing torn from her, and may be struck but not injured.

Moral law is not to be found in Homer, nor to any greater degree those of Eros. But the poet's contemporaries do not know the depraved activities later to be introduced by Asia and the gymnastic institutions. Woman is the single object of man's affections; but for her, love is restrained to the desires created in her by Venus' waist-band, "where we find all the charms and words that capture even the soul of the wise-man." Violent passions aroused by love are of another age, and will be sung by other poets.

If Andromache and Penelope are Homer's ideal of wifely devotion, he does not know Alcestis, Laodamia or Evadny, each dying for her husband or not wanting to outlive him. Clytemnestra, Antaeus, Phaedra, Alcmena and all the women either carried off or seduced by heroes and gods, are indications of men's indulgences for weaknesses they so often provoked at this time.

The captives formed a kind of harem for their masters. Many of them were to be found in Priam's palace, athough "the august Hecuba," like Penelope in Ithaca, shared the title and honors of wife and queen with no one. At home, Ulysses had fifty captives, and there is jealousy in his anger at those who abandon him for the suitors. When, before revealing himself, he hears their laughter and shouts of joy, "his heart grumbles," and he would like to kill them on the spot; but this would spoil his plans. Striking his chest he whispers "Patience, oh my heart! Have you not already suffered the cruelest of agonies?" With the suitors dead, he has twelve of the guilty hung: it is a harem scene.

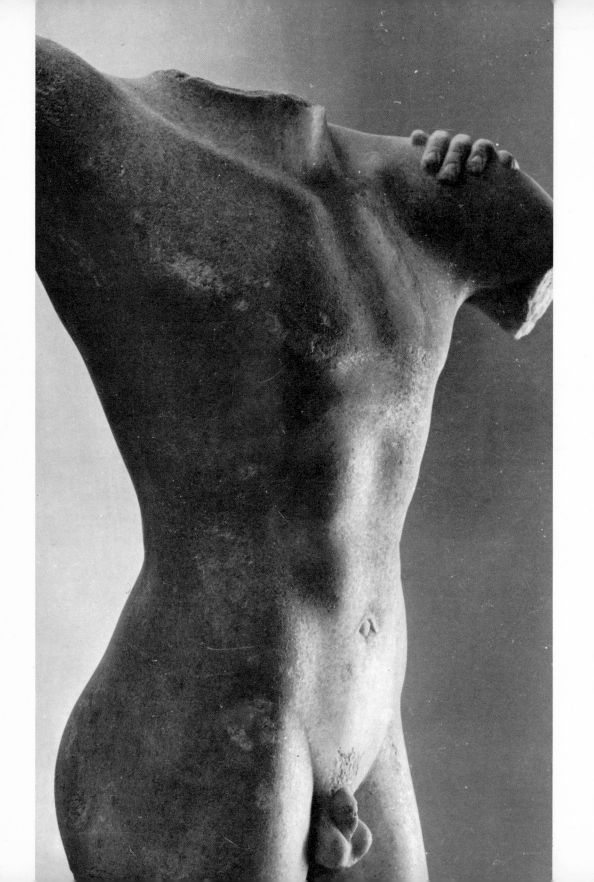

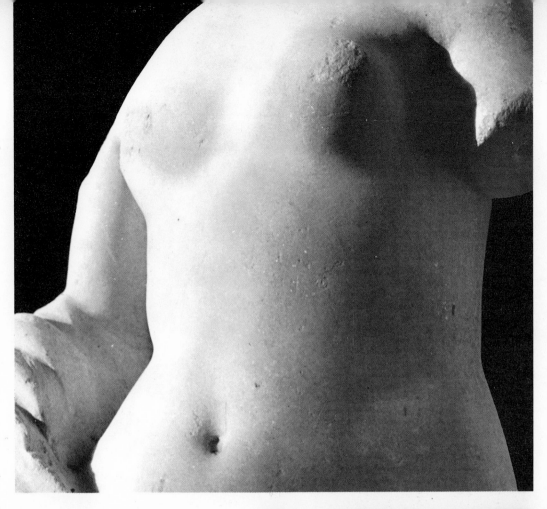

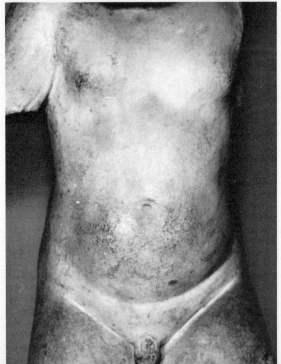

"*The desires created by Venus and her sash, containing all the charms capable of captivating even the wise man's soul...*"

"Family ties were strong, and the father's authority was respected."

Despite these most famous examples, family ties were strong, and paternal authority was respected, even by elderly sons, since a father's curse bore with it overwhelming disaster.

With the aid of Homer and Hesiod we can trace the picture of knowledge and arts possessed by the early Greeks. They had only a wooden plough to till the earth, requiring only an abundant crop of barley and a few vegetables such as peas, beans and onions, a bit of wheat, some wine, oil and honey, and some figs, olives, pears, apples and pomegranates. Grains were tread upon by oxen to bury them under the earth; flour was hand-milled between flat stones by women; bunches of grapes were dried in the sun or put in the press; oil was used only in cooking or for anointing the body. The common diet was barley cakes, vegetables and fresh or salted fish; except

on holidays and at sacrifices, very little wheaten bread or fresh meat was eaten. They knew how to shear the lamb and make fabric from wool; they worked gold, silver, copper, and more rarely iron, which was difficult to export; their weapons were in bronze, and on a value scale, bronze was to gold as nine is to one hundred. Emblems decorated chiefs' shields, and it was with the spear, struck at close range, that they conquered the long-bows of Asia. Money was still unknown: a bull served as a basis of comparison in exchanges. A captive, skillful in needlework, was worth four; the young and beautiful Eurycleia cost twenty such for Laërtes, and Lycaön in turn bought her at the price of one hundred oxen. They could build vast and solid constructions, but they did not know how to cut marble.

The centaur Chiron had discovered or learned the medical properties of certain

12

plants; Podalire's and Machaon's entire science consisted of incisions and an external medication. Later on, Aesculapius himself believed less in medication than in sweet songs and mystical words for relieving pain. In this aspect, medicine was part of religion, and doctors a kind of religious corporation.

Despite the Trojan war and the Argonauts' journey, navigation and the art of boat-building were in their infancy. Some constellations had already been named: the Great Bear and the Lesser Bear, the Pleiads, the Hyades, Orion, the Dog Star, and "Hesperus (Venus), the most brilliant star crossing the heavens."

The most ancient history of the Greeks constantly leads us back to Asia, from which they derived the majority of their gods. Some of their art processes and certain very old standards can be considered oriental imitations.

A legend, that of the Cretan Minos, understood in general terms, confirms these ancient relationships between Greece and Asia.

This wise king, the legend says, the most powerful prince of this time, reigned in Crete, whose peoples he had united under his rule, and on which he had founded three cities: Knossos, Cydonia and Phœstos. In fact, his laws were based on the foreign principle of oriental legislation in which all citizens are equal. If what we attribute to him was not a later import from a Dorian

"In the early times the Greeks had only a wooden plough to till the earth."

colony, he would have forbidden private property and made common tables, set up in public places, include all inhabitants. In time of war, his power was unlimited; in peace time a senate governed the state. Only slaves worked the land. Young Cretans, free from such labor, were subjected to a severe education whose goal was to develop the powers and inspire the qualities which create useful citizens.

Minos was also a conqueror; he built a navy and rid the Archipelago of infesting pirates. All the islands, from Thrace to Rhodes, recognized his power, and the colonies he set up on some of them, or which he established on the Asian coast, assured its continuance. Megara and Attica paid tribute to him. An expedition launched on Sicily was a failure, in which Minos was killed. There is however, the city of Minoa on this island, which carries his name. His tomb was placed beside a sanctuary to Venus, Astarte of Tyre, whose

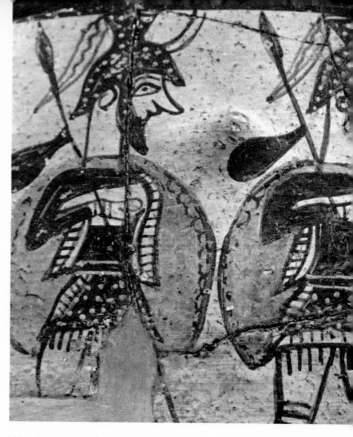

Warriors of ancient times, from a vase dating from 1200 B.C.

At Phaestos, on Crete: entrance to the Queen's bath chamber

worship the Phoenicians had passed on to him, as well as to the island of Cythera. To reward his goodness, Jupiter charged him along with his own two brothers, Aeacus and Rhadamanthus, with judging the shadows of the dead in Hell.

Later on the many adventures attributed to Minos became confusing, and due to the writers who wanted to give a legend the appearance of history. A second such character was created and made to exist a generation after Crete's law-maker, a second Minos under whom the clever Daedelus would have figured, and who would have constructed the Labyrinth to trap the Minotaur, which Theseus killed with the help of Ariadne. Under Minos II, Crete was a greater power than Greece; but after him, this power was destroyed: Idomenus, the

The bay of Assini. It is the "sure and sheltered port", according to Homer, from which the ships left for the Trojan war.

grandson of the first king, led only eighty ships against the Trojans.

While making no precise decisions about the history of Minos, we may deduce, however, according to these many traditions, the undeniable fact that Crete was indeed a great power in the early history of Greece.

In the history of the globe's development, we can clearly notice an insular period which precedes the appearance of the great continents. In Greece's history, it was also a time when the most activity was centered on the islands and the coasts of the Aegean Sea. Crete, in the midst of this activity, controlled it and gave it its greatest power.

Following pages: Memories of a flourishing Crete.

15

Pavilions of the royal palace of Cnossos and a giant vase, on Crete. "Under Minos, Crete was Greece's greatest force."

Left: Arrangement of blocks from Aphrodite's Temple on Delos. Above: a threshold. Notice the door's trace left on the ground. Below: left, a bathtub, found on the second story of a house. (These two photos taken on Delos.) Right: piece of water-distribution system found in Athens.

3 - Sparta, Athens and the other States

From the great mass of Arcadia's mountains, the Taygetus and Parnon ranges break away and stretch to the south as far as Cape Teanarus and Cape Malea, which are often struck by storms. "When you go around Cape Malea," the sailors said, "forget everything you've left at home." Between these two mountain chains flows the Eurotas River, rushing below Sparta, where it meets a slightly inclined plain which slows down its course as it continues to the sea.

A valley, closed in by the wall-like slopes of the surrounding mountains, irregularly broken by numerous hills, and in summer burned by the almost tropical sun, unaffected by sea winds while above we can see the peaks of Taygetus, often covered with snow: this is the Lacedaemon Valley.

The character and climate of this region naturally produced energetic, hardy men. The land is not infertile, but it yields its fruits only in return for the most painful labors.

Lycurgus was Sparta's great man. Research and criticisn have not been able to dispel the many uncertainties which revolve around him.

It is believed he was born in the 9th century B.C., the son of King Eunomos who, in trying to separate men in battle, received and then died of a knife wound. His older brother also met an untimely death, and Lycurgus was king until the pregnancy of the queen, his sister-in-law, was noticed; she offered to destroy the child if he would marry her. But Lycurgus outwitted her and saved his brother's son. The lords, irritated by his wise administration during Charilaos' childhood, forced him into exile. He traveled for a long time, studying with wisemen and learning the habits of foreign countries. On Crete he was instructed in the laws of Minos by a poet who sung his verses accompanied by a lyre, later calling him to Sparta to help calm the spirits. From Asia Minor he took only the poetry of Homer, but Egyptian priests counted him among their disciples. Later Spartans said that he went as far as India to learn the ancient wisdom of the Brahmins. These were long and difficult trips for the men of these times; Lycurgus did not make them, and Indian priests taught him nothing.

Upon his return, after an absence which supposedly lasted eighteen years, Lycurgus found Sparta in great trouble; the people themselves felt a great need for reform. Thus the moment was favorable. In order to add the name of Delphic Apollo, the national god, to his own authority, he consulted the

Ancient statue (found in Athens).

The Spartan plain, with the Despot's palace in the foreground.

oracle on his projects. Pythia hailed him in the name of Jupiter. Strengthened by the god's support, whether earned or bought, Lycurgus began by interesting a numerous and powerful group in his plans.

The senate was composed of thirty members. It deliberated on proposals to present to the population and judged criminal cases. Its members were elected in one way: the candidates filed past the people one by one, and each was received with greater or lesser cheers. Elders, shut in a neighboring chamber from which they could see nothing, noted those who were received with the greatest cheers, and these were then declared senators. Named for life, they were irremovable and irresponsible, which helped to give them an aristocratic

nature. The great preoccupation of legislators and politicians in antiquity was to maintain the city within its framework, without allowing it to shrink or grow beyond this. But among a small, warring people, where each citizen is an active soldier, a battle can reduce the population, and one must think rather of the prevention of exhausting the human forces; the legislator provides for this by punishments carried out on the unmarried, and by a kind of dishonor for those citizens without children. One day, Dercyllidas, a general with a great reputation, goes before an assembly; a young Lacedaemonian does not rise as he approaches, as was the custom; the old warrior is astonished. "You have no children," says the young man, "who can one day pay me the same honor." He is not considered guilty. Later on the government gave rewards to the citizens with the greatest number of children, and favored adoptions and marriages between wealthy heiresses and poor citizens. Kings who had to sanction all adoptions and arranged the marriages of orphans when the father had not made his own will known, could also, during a certain time, save a useful citizen from poverty and prevent an accumulation of wealth in the same hands.

Thus, each citizen owes the nation children. In the case of a sterile union, the wife can be loaned to fulfill one's obligation to give the state its future soldiers, a debt in which the children belong more to the city than to the father. Leaving the mother's breast, the young Spartan falls into the hands of the state; the father must bring him to the Leschia, the reunion place of the elders. Hopelessly he would try to save his son: if the elders find him weak or unfit, he is thrown from the top of Mount Taygetus, and the poor child is punished by death the first day of his life for not promising to be a sturdy enough warrior, a cruel and monstrous custom accepted as a necessity by philosophers and politicians starting with Plato and Aristotle.

After this terrible inspection of those who are forced to be part of it, the state gives the child back to his mother and allows him to remain with her until he is seven years old; at this age it then reclaims him, never again to release him, and from this moment on, the child's life is a long trial of patience. sobriety and even suffering. He is immediately placed in a troop in which teachers, chosen from among the best of the young men, direct under the surveillance of an officer called a *pedonome*. They are trained in the palaestra or gymnasium, in running and the use of weapons, anything that will increase the force and agility of their bodies; their minds are trained in courage and patience. "You will have great difficulty," said Xenophon, "in finding better formed

These statues recall the Greeks of ancient times.

men and more lissom bodies than the Spartans: they give equal care to the exercising of the neck, the hands and the legs. They wear no shoes, and the same garment is worn summer and winter; for a bed they use reeds they themselves cut in the Eurotas; they are given little nourishment in order to force them to pilfer by cunning and shrewdness what they must to satisfy their appetites." It is unusual to see theft taught in such a way; but because of the society uniting the Spartans, it is not truly theft. One who allows himself to be caught is punished, not as a guilty party, but as a clumsy one. In war, they will thus remember in tracking the enemy, the clever devices learned as children for finding food. To harden them to suffering, they are made to undergo rugged ordeals, and they are beaten with rods at the altar of Diana, the one best bearing the pain being awarded the title of "victor of the altar."

The Lacedaemonians' education was just slightly less grueling. Instead of commiting them to a sedentary life in the gynaeceum, women slaves were made to spin wool and make clothing; young Spartan girls were to maintain themselves in order to one day give robust children to the nation. For them, as for the young Spartan men, there were exercises for the body, races, wrestling, keeping them healthy and strong. The Phenomerides went nearly naked before the citizens until they were twenty years old, the normal age of marriage. The Spartans were of necessity strong-willed and austere of habit. There was no luxury: this principle was maintained by money made of heavy iron, whose smallest sum needed to be carried in a chariot, and which was worthless outside the region.

Commerce, like its consequent luxury, was shunned. Foreigners would have brought new ideas: they were in fact forbidden to enter Sparta, except on certain days. Nor could a Spartan voyage outside the region without an official permission, and the

"The Spartans must have had strict habits."

death penalty was proscribed for those who tried to live in another land: they were deserters.

The same principle was applied to the institution of common meals, to which all Spartans, even kings, were obliged to attend under the penalty of losing his political rights, unless the absentee was excused for purposes of a sacrifice or a prolonged hunt, which promised the guests a present for the feast. These meals, called *phidities,* were strict; each man was provided with an equal amount of barley flour, wine, wheat, figs, and small share of seasoning or meat. One could add to this only hunted game or a part of the sacrifices burned for the gods. Anyone who was so poor as to bring nothing was excluded from the tables and lost his rights as a citizen.

The dish which began the meal was the black broth which made Dionysius of

"Attica is the most justifiably celebrated place in the world in the history of the human mind." — "The horizon which draws the eye far out into the Aegean Sea..."

Syracuse make a face. "Something is really missing in here," said the cook who had prepared it for him. "What then?" "Your having gone for a swim in the Eurotas." Old men as well as children attended these meals; heroic deeds were praised here, and shameful actions were blasted, all with sharp but friendly mockery.

In times of war, guests at the same table became soldiers in the same regiment, so that each man, fighting in sight of his friends, was encouraged and strengthened.

Each citizen could punish the children of another citizen. When necessary, one could borrow a neighbors' slaves, his hunting dogs, or his horses, on the condition that he return everything to its place in the same state that he found it. The Spartans sometimes went so far in the sacrifice of personal property that they were greatly admired by

Xenophon, and would have been especially repellent to us with our ideas on the sanctity of family ties.

The small region separated from central Greece by imposing mountains and which stretches out in a promontory into the Aegean Sea, bounded on the right by Euboea, on the left by the smaller islands of Salamis and Aegina, is Attica, the most justly celebrated place in the world in the history of the human mind. It is divided into three, semi-circular basins, the plains of Eleusis, Athens and Marathon. The genius of the inhabitants, shaped by the location of the area, historic circumstances and a climate of a sweet spring and a clement winter, differs profoundly from the Spartan nature: open and vast like the limitless horizon seen from the Acropolis, drawing the eye far out into the Aegean; lively and sharp

"The inhabitants' spirit, formed by the land, historic circumstances, and a climate giving such a sweet springtime and a wild winter..."

like the sea breeze which ruffles the purpled hills of Attica; inquisitive, strong and industrious, like the minds of those who often live on the coast and see many foreigners, and whose lands are not sufficient for them; and lastly, endlessly kept on guard by the multiplicity of impressions received through the pure and sonorous air during transparent nights, which are not the darkness of shadow, but rather the absence of daylight. The Athenians were well-balanced because of the very nature of their land, where nothing was to be found in abundance; but even more important was that they had a well-balanced mind.

"Land along the shores"—this is the meaning of the name Attica, open to the sea on three sides, receiving from there and from the routes of the Beotian mountains inhabitants of very different origins. Each group took up separate quarters and refused to have anything in common with the others. Much time and effort was needed to reduce these many states to twelve, to unite them through marriages, and to have them bring their disputes before a common tribunal. This first union was called in legend Cecrops; the second, in which twelve villages made up a single city and political unit after each civil unit, was called Theseus.

Later on in Athens there was to be found a man who lived without public honors amidst the crowd of fellow-citizens. In his youth he had devoted himself to trade to make up for the injustice of his inheritance as arranged by his father. He had traveled a great deal, searching at the same time, among the many peoples who passed before his eyes, fortune by trade and science by the study of manners and matters. He had the reputation of a wise man, but a moderate wise man, who did not disdain the good things in life, good cheer and love, who even sang its pleasures in rather light verses, mixed, it is true, with good and profound maxims: his name was Solon.

Solon's genius was basically human, as was the Constitution he undertook to give to Athens.

There were three parties in the city: the men of the mountains, who wanted to change everything; the *paralians,* who wanted to change a few things; and the *pedians,* who did not want to change anything. Won over by Solon's moderation, they all agreed to put powers, responsibilities and revenues in his hands, in a word to give him dictatorship while he created the State. His friends urged him to maintain the dictatorship, and to make himself a tyrant rather than a law-maker; he responded with sharp comments and continued his work.

The government was made up of four potitical bodies: the archons, the Areopagus, the senate and the assembly.

The archons always numbered nine, and like priests, had no bodily deformity. They

25

"In Athens there was to be found a man who lived without public honors, in the midst of his fellow citizens. His name was Solon. His genius was basically human."

shared executive power and corresponded more or less to our cabinet members. They also kept their judiciary powers, excepting the appeals handled by tribunals recruited by drawing lots from all classes of the populace. When they were taken into office, they swore to uphold the laws; when they left office here, they rendered an account of their administration to the general assembly, and were admitted to the Areopagus. As long as they were on duty, their person was inviolable.

The two anchors, as Plutarch said, which held down the vessel of the State, even in a storm, were the Areopagus and the senate, or council of four hundred.

The Aeropagus, the highly respected former court of justice, met on Mars' hill, in the open air, because it could not meet under the same roof with men whose hands were supposedly impure. It judged crimes of murder, mutilation, poisoning and treason, and was made up of archons released from their former duties, consequently generally aged men, highly skilled in affairs. Solon raised it to a position of supreme court, and charged it with the responsibility of overlooking the entire city, customs, education, religion, and revising even the peoples' judgments, with the power to reinitiate an inquiry in some affair or trial.

The four hundred senators were chosen from the first classes. They prepared the laws that were to be submitted to the assembly of the people, took care of finances and administration, rendered decrees which were law for the year, and lastly, could impose certain fines.

The senate was the permanent council of the people, but the people were the only ruler. The popular assembly, called by the senate, was made up of all citizens; normally only a small number showed up at the Agora. A foreigner who might slip in before having received the city's permission was punished by death or sold as a slave, since he had encroached upon the sovereign power.

To prevent problems with trials, Solon had established that citizens sixty years old, approved by both parties could make up a court by arbitration, whose sentence would be without appeal.

A special tribunal, that of the 51 ephetes, judged involontary murders or which had been commited in cases of legitimate defense. The ephetes were all at least fifty years old and of noble birth.

The normal penalties were fines, confiscation of property, prison, and death; a special penalty, the *atimy*, took away part or all of a citizen's rights.

A law freed those who had been made slaves due to poverty, and prevented in the future a creditor from having any rights to the debtor's person. Stone signs disappeared from the fields of Attica, which had been engraved with debts; it was what we would call the paying off of mortgages. There still exist the verses in which Solon boasts of having freed the land which had been in bondage before him, and returned to their country the debtors that had been sold abroad, "who, for having erred in the world, had forgotten the Attic language."

At first there was grumbling about this law; but its wiseness was recognized; yet during the three centuries that it existed, the Athenian democracy never withdrew Solon's laws and measures, a great mark in his honor. The respect for property became so deeply rooted that one no longer dared to ask for a repeal of his debts or for depreciation of money. Solon's reform was, in fact, something quite different from a simple repeal of debts. The energetic words he used to describe it led one to believe that he was doing away with an agricultural problem, analogous to that of the Roman farmers; and a word from Aristotle confirms this idea: "Solon stopped the slavery of people."

The peace that came of these measures gave Solon more freedom of spirit for his other laws. In them he used the same moderation, and forced himself to reconcile principles and opposing interests, uniting, as he said, strength and justice.

Above all he declared an amnesty which excluded only murderers and traitors. He created two major innovations: by the first, each citizen took a certain part in the rights implied by the title; by the second, the

"The popular assembly was made up of all citizens: usually only a small number of them showed up at the agora."— An orator, from a vase of the period, and a view of the remains of the agora.

population was divided into four classes according to wealth. Thus the first leaned the State toward democracy; the second was still democratic, in that it abolished special priviledges for the nobility, but it was also aristocratic in the sense that it placed wealthy people in charge of the State.

Four classes were organized in the following way: the first included all the citizens who had an annual income of at least 500 drachmas, in dry or liquid products, and for this reason were called *pentacisiomedimnes*. Positions as archons, important responsibilities and the command of the army and navy were reserved for them.

The second class was composed of *cavaliers,* that is to say those who had an income of at least 300 drachmas, the amount deemed necessary to maintain a horse. This class became the cavalry; several lesser functions were given it.

The third was that of the *zeugites,* or owners of a team of oxen, which was equivalent to an income of 150 to 200 drachmas. It made up the heavily armed infantry; some minimal responsibilities were reserved for them.

Finally the fourth class included, under the title of *thetes* or mercenaries, all those who had less than 150 drachmas in real property, whatever their personal wealth might be. They formed the light troops and navy, receiving a salary drawn by the state from the upper classes. They were excluded from responsibilities and honors, but accepted in the assembly of the people and the tribunals.

This inequality in the division of honors was compensated by the way in which taxes were organized. The fourth class did not pay any at all, while the first three were taxed according to Solon's idea that a citizen's duties to the community increase with his wealth. They paid in proportion to the nominal value attributed to their property; but while this value was estimated for the first class at par with the real value,

for the second it was reduced by a sixth, and for the third, four ninths. Thus a property giving 500 drachmas in income was estimated at 12 times this amount, that is, 6,000 drachmas or one talent, while the cavalier's property, rather than be valued at 12 times 300, or 3,600, was only 3,000, at those of the *zeugites* at 1,000 rather than 1,800. This advantage was more specious than actual, since the direct tax on income was used only in cases of great necessity, while the indirect tax on imported merchandise was permanent and was paid by the poor as well as the rich.

Every citizen had the right to bring a proposition before the people, but no one, not even the archons, could do it with the senate as intermediary. Every citizen also had the right to speak in the assembly, from the time he was twenty years old; but fifty-year-old men spoke first, a minor privilege given to old age, and greatly inferior to complete power it had in Sparta. Did it give enough care to the experience of age? Was not too much attention given to the impetuosity of youth? A century and a half later, Aristophanes bitterly complained of the Athenians disdain for the elderly. It must be said however that custom ruled more severely than rights, and normally one only saw the state orators at the tribunal, ten citizens who, after public examination, were charged with the defense of the Republic's interests. Thus it was a very influential function, and one of the most honored. Every citizen had the right to bring an orator to justice, if his life was not irreproachable; if he had been a bad son or a bad soldier, or if he proposed a decree contrary to existing laws. In this last case, an action was brought against him in the name of the old laws, and the orator could be punished by exile or a ruinous fine. When he was in the tribunal, he wore a myrtle crown upon his head, as did the senators and magistrates: it was the symbol of citizens acting in the interest of the State.

The number necessary to render valid a decision in the Assembly was not fixed, except in certain cases where 6,000 citizens were minimum. Thucydides remarks that there were rarely as many as 5,000 members at an ordinary Assembly; the reason is that the Athenians were not an oligarchic association like the Spartans. In Attica one had to earn his daily bread by agriculture, industry or commerce. Moreover the law which prohibited idleness and obliged each citizen to declare each year the profession by which he lived, was made to enforce the habit of working. Later it was even necessary to pay the people for their attendance at the Assembly. When the Athenian idler stopped to chatter in the market place, while the senators and the faithful attenders waited in the Pnyx in vain, Scythians, paid by the State to be the city's police, went out in search of him. They went through the streets and the markets, carrying vermillion cord, marking those who were late, and who could no longer come up to the *lexiarch* to get their attendance voucher. As the Scythians approached, it was a contest as to who ran the fastest, trying to avoid them and arrive on time within the sacred walls. What must it have been for these gay, turbulent people during a long session of the Assembly, where it was forbidden, under penalty of fine, to leave before the end!

In a palace of Crete.

4 - Youths and Citizens, Metics and Slaves

Many Greek cities had forbidden celibacy; in the *Laws,* Plato says that the citizen who has not married by the time he is thirty-five years old must be fined 100 drachmas a year, and that he may not expect the honors from the young that are normally due to the elderly. We do not know if Solon needed to take such strict measures. During his time, religion was still obeyed, and since it demanded that the domestic household always have offerings, dead libations (this will be explained further on), it imposed marriage.

Since young ladies lived very much hidden from the public, marriage was chiefly an agreement between parents, taking place most often in the months of January and February, the time Nature begins to awaken from her winter sleep. This solemnity was always accompanied by religious ceremonies: first there were sacrifices in honor of the protective gods of marriage; then the nuptial bath in the holy water, drawn by the girls from the fountain of Kallirrhoe. After the fiancée's last meal in the paternal home, she awaited her husband, dressed in festival clothes, who fetched her and with her on a chariot, followed the procession of young girls singing the epithalamium or nuptial song.

Abortion was frequent; the Hippocratic Oath, in which doctors swore not to prevent it, is proof, and recommends it for keeping the population from going beyond a certain fixed point.

One must not think that Greek marriage was a religious act devoid of sentiment and affection. This would assume that the ancients had natures very different from ours. It is true that then, as today, legislators concerned themselves with rites and not

30

The seductress...

The seducer... Right: a couple in love.

"*A procession of young girls singing the epithalamium...*"

sentiments, but Solon has defined marriage in terms which are very much our own: "An intimate union between man and wife, having as its goals the founding of a new family and the tasting together of the sweets of mutual tenderness." His laws for dowries followed this. The fiancée had to bring to her husband only three dresses and a few pieces of furniture of little value. Concerned about womens' dignity, he limited their freedom in favor of decency; he regulated their travels, their mourning, their sacrifices; he forbade them from leaving the city with more than three dresses, or carrying more than one obolus worth of goods at a time, and from traveling in the city streets at night, except on a chariot preceded by a flame. He consecrated an old family right: if a young girl was an orphan, the closest relative on the father's side had to marry her, or provide her with a dowry based on his own property and

"Solon forbade women to leave the city with more than three dresses."

find a husband for her. But he abolished the unnatural law authorizing the citizen to sell his son or daughter, or his sister or his ward, unless the latter deserved such severity by her conduct.

The family retains a certain mystery here, respected and not exposed naked in daylight as in Lacedaemon; nor was it engulfed, as it later would be by the Romans, in *pater familias*. In Athens, the strength of marriage and motherhood are merely means of protection and defense. Solon even did away with the father's ancient right

32

to sell or kill his son. Rather, the child grew up in the arms of his parents, without the State's interfering indiscreetly in the family sanctuary. From this resulted, from both father and son, special relationships and duties, quite in accord with Nature. In Sparta, the son had no more respect for his father than for any other elder citizen; in his eyes his father was merely another elderly member of the State. In Athens, Solon unknowingly repeats what Plato will later say in the *Decalogue:* "Honore the gods and respect those who gave you life." He obliges the grown son to care for the sick father, and before allowing a citizen to take an important office, it checked to see

"Solon took away the father's ancient right of selling or killing his child."

"From their sixteenth year on they were in the charge of the gymnasium."

if he had been a good son, and if he honored his parents during their life and after their death.

Until sixteen years of age, the parents raised the child in the manner they chose; Aristotle disapproved of this custom because the parents' education was often weak, capricious and contributed to the weakening of the city. From his sixteenth year, the child was sent to the gymnasium, or to the Hermes *Hegemonios,* one who conducted and presided over the lessons. One did not try to fill the child's mind with a mass of knowledge that

33

"The taste for harmony that music can give... (the search for) force, skill and beauty..."

At Delos: the Nymph's body, at the Museum, and a statue among the ruins of a temple.

burdened the memory without developing intelligence. Their education was divided into two series of studies: the *Gymnastic,* or danse, wrestling and gymnastic contests for the body; and the *Teaching of the Muses,* for the soul. They lived with poets who knew all the heroic and sacred legends, and advantageous proverbs; with Homer, Hesiod and the lyric poets; with the gnomics, who had gathered all human wisdom; and one tried to inspire their minds with the order at the base of Greek literature, as well as the taste of harmony that music can instill; but they were not overloaded with long and tedious studies which would weaken or ruin their physical constitution. Thus, for this double being, a double education: on one side "the gifts of Apollo and the Muses;" on the other, exercises favorable to developing force, dexterity and beauty; such was the system followed with the hope of creating men, citizens and soldiers.

At the end of his eighteenth year, the child was of civil age; the young man could claim his inheritance; it is written in the book of *ephebes* that he will now start his political and military novitiate. Each year, Athenians of this age were before the altar called "the common home of the people," and in the presence of the exegetists, those in charge of interpreting oracles, and the priest of the Graces, whose duty it was to invoke the protection of the gods for the city, the *ephebe* took the following oath: "I shall not dishonor the sacred arms given to me by my country, and I will not desert my companion in arms. I will fight for all that is good and holy, alone or among many; I will give my country in return no less than I have received from it, but greater and stronger. I will obey officers and laws, and if someone destroys these laws, or does not obey them, I will take vengeance, alone or with my fellow-citizens, and I will honor the religion of my fathers. I take the gods as witness to my oath."

With this heroic oath the *ephebes* were

Left: an ephebe of a rich family (with a servant); above: two ephebes conversing.

placed in the surveillance of a yearly officer, the *cosmet*. They attended classes in philosophy, music, eloquence and poetry, these to form their minds; religious festivals because worship and one's country were so closely tied; assemblies of the people in order to study public affairs; gymnastic exercises to make their bodies lissom and strong; lastly, as war apprentices, they served as police in the interior and as guards in the fortresses on the seacoast.

Since there was always the possibility of the city's being attacked, and since there were no machines to defend the ramparts, strong, active and unyielding men were needed for hand to hand combat, men whose determined spirits were prepared to make all sacrifices the country demanded.

At twenty, one came of political age; the young man became a citizen in the full meaning of the word; he could vote in the general assembly, and, as it was said, could take the floor to speak.

At thirty the citizen could become a member of the senate. At sixty he was discharged from military service and could retire.

The same laws applied under adoption as for a natural son.

For a long time, working the fields and growing crops were the citizens' principal occupations, even for the rich.

Thus Solon did not need to prescribe conditions in favor of agriculture. Rather he wanted to encourage industry and trade, wishing each citizen to have a trade.

In order to keep commodities at a low price, he prohibited the exportation of all products from the earth, excepting olive oil; this then encouraged industry.

The foreigner established in Athens bore the name of *metic* (one who lives with). He personally contributed 12 drachmas as the head of a family, in return for the State's protection, and if he failed to pay this, he was sold as a slave. Such would have been

"*For a long time, the working of the fields and the keeping of crops were the main occupations of citizens, even the rich ones.*"

"*Solon forbade the exportation of the products of the earth, except for olive oil.*" *Below, left: an ancient olive press. Right: in an oil store of a no longer extant urban center, a small channel allows for the collecting of the spilled liquid.*

the case of the philosopher Xenocrates, if a rich citizen had not recognized him as he passed the auction market and paid his debt. The tax for a foreign woman was half as much; a son's tax exempted his mother, just as a husband's exempted his wife. The same conditions were applied to freed men. The *metic* had to choose a patron from among the citizens who would answer for his conduct and was his pledge. Once these obligations were fulfilled, he was free to trade and exercise his profession. But the *metics* could not acquire property, and a custom was initiated which gave them certain degrading duties during the festivals; thus in the processions they carried vases and sacred implements, and their wives carried parasols over the heads of the Athenian matrons. Xenophon later wanted these irritating distinctions abolished; and in effect, during the long wars, many were accepted into the ranks of citizens, and the *metic's* general condition was improved. And they deserved it, having taken their share of the risks in the country's dangers, serving as rowers in the navy or as soldiers, and even in its land armies as hoplites, in the midst of the national troops.

The same liberal spirit held true concerning slaves, and for the same reasons. Solon wanted that those who were mistreated by their masters demand to be sold, thus passing under a less severe authority. The law guaranteed them a defender; and while awaiting judgment, the temple of Theseus was an inviolable refuge. No one was allowed to strike them. Their death was considered an outrage, and was treated as if the victim had been a free man. According to Xenophon, this was the reason: "If custom allowed a free man to strike a slave, a foreigner or a freed man, the citizen could often be the victim of error. There is nothing, either in deportment or dress which distinguishes the foreigner or the slave."

Athens was repaid for this kindness. Never, even during its most difficult periods,

A stick in hand: it is a wealthy person.

did it ever see a revolt of the servile class, which so often in Sparta and Rome had taken a cruel toll. The revolt of the slaves employed in the Laurium mines was an isolated, local incident. Yet even in Athens, slaves as well as *metics* were forbidden to practice music or gymnastics, considered proper for free men only. Freed men could pass into the *metic* class, but could not become citizens. And accused of ingratitude by his patron, the freed man could be put back into his original class. "Be a slave," said the law, "because you do not know how to be free."

The State had public slaves: these were a corps of archers called Scythians, who policed the streets, guarded the prison and executed the condemned. Their number later rose from three hundred to six hundred, to velve hundred, and some of them were even nployed in the army.

It must be said however that the

Athenian slave did not escape all the miseries of servitude. The Greeks, having no machines to carry out the most rugged jobs, the slaves did the work, and, like everywhere else, he was under his master's will, whatever it called for. In the case of a trial, free citizens, who could not be tortured, sent their own slaves under the pretext of seeing justice done. "Take my slave and may he be tortured," says a character in Aristophanes. The torturer's arsenal was very well furnished with everything that made the flesh cry out. That the unfortunate man died in the torture was unimportant: the master beaten in the trial paid his adversary an indemnity for the dead slave.

We know that the Athenians were acquainted with eunuchs. We prefer to believe that they were bought in Asia, and that they themselves did not practice this custom.

All purchased women did not stay at home to spin wool and take care of domestic chores. Their masters had the right to abuse them, and make a profit on their charms by placing them in certain houses; it was a high-paying industry. But if the slave was the ugly wound of the ancient world, at least his condition was a bit better in Athens than elsewhere; and we can not ask more of the Athenians.

With his legislation, Solon established solid ties among the citizens. They owed each other mutual protection; one who witnessed an outrage to another citizen was obliged to report it immediately to the judges; in the case of murder, the parents of the deceased had to demand the punishment of the guilty of the court. Lastly, to destroy political indifference, which in a Republic is a deadly evil, he made this special law: "All citizens will take arms in a civil war."

When Solon's laws were published, they were engraved on turning, wooden rollers, placed on the Acropolis, so that they would be constantly seen by the people. But he was so often assailed with questions, with pleas to interpret certain laws, that he asked his fellow citizens for permission to go off, after having had the senators and archons swear that they would maintain his laws unchanged for ten years. He then visited Egypt, where the priests spoke to him of Atlantis, this great island in the Ocean which had disappeared under the waves.

Each of us should recall this phrase of his: "I grow old by always learning." But he added: "What I love still are the gifts of Cyprian Venus, Bacchus and the Muses."

It was later on that ostracism was established. In Athens each year, during the sixth month, the following question was debated in the senate and before the assembly: "Does the safety of the State demand a vote of ostracism?" If this necessity was recognized, the people would be called to vote on it. No name was spoken, but the name of the citizen deemed necessary to send from the city was written on a seashell covered in wax, thus maintaining equality and preventing the possibility of an assumption of rights. It was a secret vote, and the archons counted them. The citizen designated so by the majority was banished for ten years. And, as in the case of the exile, his property was not confiscated.

A word on Greece's secondary states. They were of considerable number. Each one of them had its own history, having had its own life, but this history is far from clear. In addition, its interior life was generally a repetition of what we have seen in Athens and Sparta; and most often in its exterior life it was linked with those of the two main Republics.

Neighboring on Attica, separated from it only by the gorges of the Parnes, Boeotia has an entirely different aspect: there is much more vegetation here; the land, rich and fed by many streams, seems lush and fertile; pasture-land is abundant; but in this fertile region one searches in vain for the harmonious contours of Attica; the

Ostracism: "The people wrote the name of the citizen whom it judged necessary to remove from the city on a shell covered in wax."

mountains' contours are less precise, their peaks not as sharp; and one's horizon seems limited in all directions.

The Boeotian cities formed a league among themselves, at the head of which was Thebes; but this pre-eminence ended in absolute domination.

All antiquity mocked the Boeotians' stupidity. And yet they gave Greece its most famous lyric poet, Pindar, his rival Corinna, and the one placed closest to Homer in great poetry, Hesiod.

Opposite, on the other side of the Euripus, stretches a monstrously long island, Euboea, a land rich in grazing herds. Its Eastern coast is steep and without ports; its other coast, on the contrary, easily accesible at thousands of points, opens toward the center into a large fertile plain, where the islands two main cities, Eretria and Chalcis, were built.

The Chalcidians were famous for a vice practiced by Greece in general, which it transmitted to the Roman Empire and which the East has kept. On the public square, they had built a lavish monument linked to both an heroic tradition and the memory of this amorous chivalry whose object was not women.

Arcadia, behind its chain of high mountains, has a tormented surface, where except for the valley of the Ladon, the waters chartered no specific course and run helter-skelter over the land in all directions.

The history of this land, so drenched with sun, is incomplete. A multitude of villages scattered throughout these endless valleys lived in isolation here. But thanks to its poverty and isolation, Arcadia escaped the revolutions which so often wrecked the populations of the other regions of Greece. "The Arcadians," said Pausanias, have occupied from the start as they do today,

"This amorous chivalry of which women were not the object..."

the same land." They themselves supposed that they were older than the moon, and they spoke the oldest dialect in Greece, Aeolic. Their mountains with their sharp peaks, still stand guard over the remains of gigantic fortresses made of enormous blocks of stone. Their chief god was Jupiter. His altar was a mound of earth; his temple was a sanctuary made from uncut rocks and human sacrifices were made here. Strangers were not allowed to enter. He who did so infallibly died within the year. To assure the truth of this oracle, the inhabitants, when they could catch him, stoned the guilty man to death within the hour. In all of Arcadia, Jupiter shared his honors and temples with another very popular divinity in this province, and whose worship was probably older: Pan, the protector of shepherds and their flocks of both male and female goats, from whom he borrowed lascivious habits, but was at the same time the god of fire, who spreads life on earth by making Ceres' crops grow, and for this reason was called the Great Mother's attendant. Yet at times the Arcadians treated him with little respect: when the hunt was poor, they gave great blows with a whip to his statue. Pan, the god of deep forests, which the winds filled with mysterious noises, and where light and shadow created fantastic images, was the reason for sudden, causeless fears; his terror was *panic*.

Corinth had unfertile land, but as a means of defense had an impregnable acropolis on a steep mass of rock, 1,750 feet high, and as its wealth, two ports on two seas: the Archipel and the Ionian sea; Leche, in the West, was attached to the city by a strong, high, defensive wall, about 7,200 feet long. The difficulties of navigating around the Peloponnesus was the fortune of the city which, by its ports, connected the Saronic Gulf with that of Corinth, and could, according to its will, open or close the isthmus which bears its name. This isthmus, which Pindar called a bridge over the abyss, is

only three to four miles wide, and the
land is almost level, or at least, in its lower
part, has only uniform slopes rising by
gradual degrees to an altitude of 200 to
250 feet. The Corinthians were also able to
build a road, the Diolcos, for ships which,
placed on rollers, crossed, with the aid of a
machine, from one sea to the other.

Corinth's prosperity dates from earliest
time, Thucydides said that ancient poets
called Corinth the rich one. The first
trireme was constructed there around 700
B.C. To protect its trade it policed the
surrounding seas for pirates, and in 664 B.C.,
led against the Corcyrians, who had
quickly forgotten their origins, the oldest
known naval combat in the time of Thucydides. Corinth was also the first to mold
figures, and led the other Greek states in the
art of design. Later it gave its name to the
richest of architectural orders. In its
workshops the finest wool was spun, the most
well-known bronzes were created, its painted
vases were desired everywhere, and its
perfumes rivaled those of the Orient. But
the frequent visits of its ships in the ports
of the eastern sea, and the great number of
foreigners within its walls developed, along
with industry and luxury, the superstitions
and vices found in Asiatic cities. Like the
Syriac and Babylonian cities, it had many
priestesses of Venus.

*Above:
site of the ruins of Corinth. "Poets called
Corinth the rich one." Below: men leaning
on a table...*

Left: a street in ancient Greece.

5 - Gods and Heroes

Greek gods are forces of Nature or manifestations of moral or physical activity; but they are also good and bad men, just as we are; and it is because they represent humanity that they lived so long a time.

Herodotus regards the poems of Homer and Hesiod as the source of all religious beliefs in Greece. The amiable narrator tells us that he posed these impertinent questions to the priestesses of Dodona:"Where did each god come from? Did they all exist always? What shape do they take?" And he adds: "It is only recently that one has been able to answer these questions, perhaps because Homer and Hesiod are barely four hundred years older than me. And it is they who created the theogony of the Greeks, giving them their names, their honors and their forms."

Among the rites and legends of heroes and gods, we find the oldest worship of forests, the adoration of mountains, rocks, winds, and rivers. Agamemnon, in the Iliad, still invokes them like great divinities, and Achilles offers his fine head of hair to the Simois River. During the entire life of Hellenism, the oak was consecrated to Jupiter, the laurel to Apollo, the olive tree to Minerva, the myrtle to Venus, etc. Serpents, after having played a threatening role in earlier times, became the beneficent spirits at Delphi, Epidaurus and Athens. Lastly, certain rocks had divine images. Thus Hercules was represented at Hyettos in Boeotia by an uncut stone; Jupiter at Tegea by a triangular rock; and there were many others.

The worship of fire is connected to the beliefs of primitive times, that which burned in the home, those of the gods' altars and the States, and that which sprang mysteriously from the depths of volcanic lands.

"The Earth produces fruits, honor it with the name of Mother". It was called Mother Earth, from which was derived the name Demeter.

The Pelasgians, the Greeks' ancestors, seem to have honored the Supreme Being, with neither temple nor image. "For a long time," says Heorodotus, "they did not know the name of any god." The snowy peaks of mountains served as an altar for the one which, being the pure light of the sky, would become Zeus, "the Shining." When they wanted him to draw near to them, they called him lively names, Zeus Pater, from which comes the Roman name Jupiter. His worship dominated in three or four places which history shows us to be the oldest inhabited spots in Greece: at Dodona in Epirus, where the oak with sweet acorns and the beech with nutritious fruit were consecrated to him; on the Lyceum, the highest peak in Arcadia, and on Mount Dictea in Crete. The Cretans willingly told of his birthplace and indicated his tomb.

This silent adoration of the"pure God," of the "God father," indicates a monotheistic

The fresco above shows worshippers offering a goat to Demeter.

Athen, Poseidon and perhaps Artemis, also entered Greece from both sides, the north and south, by land and sea. The gods naturally took this double path. These divine hosts that the Greeks called forth, on the waves of the Aegean and on the coasts of Thrace, paved their way with altars, leaving these souvenirs behind. This history of the gods becomes a counter-proof to that of man.

There are two kinds of religion: those revealed in a Holy Book, and those of Nature. Jews, Christians and Moslems have the former, while the Orient and Greece have the latter, diving into the heart of Nature, from which there flows the great current of universal life. In the religions come from Sinai, Jerusalem and Mecca, religious development came from prophets, interpreting a sacred text; in Greece, the interpreters were poets.

A bust of Zeus.

conception which would not last, but which philosophy would bring forth again. The worship of the Sky was related to that of the land. "The pure Sky," says Aeschylus, "loves to penetrate the Earth draws in this marriage. The rain falling from the sky nourishes it; it then gives mortals pastures for flock and harvests." The same thought is found in the invocation addressed to Zeus by the Peleiades of Dodona: "The Earth produces fruits, honor her with the name Mother." One said Mother-Earth, and from this came the name Demeter, one of Zeus' wives, called Ceres by the Sicilian and Italiot Greeks. At Mantinea a fire was constantly kept burning on her altar, as on Vesta's in Rome. Hymns sung in the temples called her from Crete; indeed she came from much farther away, since she was the traveling goddess who sprang harvests from beneath her step. In Eleusis, the basis of her mysteries were attributed to the Thracians. Zeus, Apollo, Dionysus,

"Poseidon or Neptune, the god of the sea..." — *We see a bust of the god here, being unearthed.*

The Phoenicians of Sidon spread the worship of their protective divinity, Astarte or Aphrodite; her image decorated the prows of their ships, to protect them from the waves, which the Greeks poetically expressed by saying that Venus was born on the white foam of the briny deep. From Ascalon she passed to Cypress, and from there to Cythera, "the empurpled island," where the Phoenicians built a temple to her. But her worship spread slowly: in the Homeric period it was still quite restricted. Later, the Syrian goddess, become the goddess of love, was the most charming creation of the religious spirit of the Greeks; she had altars everywhere, images embodying the perfect feminine beauty, and too many worshippers.

Poseidon or Neptune, the god of the sea, who demands human sacrifices and the burning of horses, must be one of the country's oldest divinities, undoubtedly

brought by the Greeks from Asia and the islands along with Rhea, the Phrygian Cybele, and Minerva (Athena). The former never played anything but a minor role in Greece, while the latter had as her symbol the olive tree, native to the Asian coasts. Olympia and Athena seem to have worshipped Poseidon earlier in a particular religion, and the Ionians considered him their national god; in Asia, general assemblies were held in his temple. On the other hand, he was not held in great honor by the Dorians, except at Corinth. Earlier legends naturally made Poseidon the husband of Demeter: the humid element nourishing the land.

At first, Athena was not the symbol of moral qualities later represented by Minerva, but a personification of the waters, which naturally connected her with Neptune, not however for the marriage, since sterile as the briny deep, she remained the barren virgin. Later she was the divinity of war whom Homer shows us covering heroes on the battlefield. But it was inevitable that the goddess of the incorruptible waters and the impalpable air should become also that of chastity and moral purity, when Greek polytheism, escaping from naturalism by the progress of ideas, became more spiritual by substituting the personification of the deadly forces of matter with the moral qualities placed in the gods as they ware gradually discovered in man himself. Thus Pallas-Athena, sprung from Jupiter's brain, like his divine thought, became the industrious goddess and the intelligent force which nothing could resist.

Dionysus (Bacchus), the god of the vine, had first appeared on the island of Naxos, and was forever worshipped by the Thracians; Artemis (Diana), the worship of homicide and wild customs, such as the Amazons, who had a famous sanctuary at Ephesus, and dreaded altars at Tauris; lastly Ares (Mars), the god of carnage and perhaps Thrace's principle divinity: all these were evidently of foreign origin.

But the most important of these religious novelties was the late introduction into Greece of the worship of Apollo, the eternally young and beautiful god, personification of the radiant light he created.

The first altars to Apollo in Hellas were built on Olympus and the rock of Delos. A third, which became far more famous than the other two, was supposed built by the Cretans at Cryssa, on the Gulf of Corinth, later transported to the cliffs of Parnassus, a majestic site, advantageous for the safety of the priests and the faith of the pilgrims. When the Olympic Dorians established themselves near Phocis, they confusedly gave the same veneration to the sanctuaries of Delphi and Tempe, and each year a religious procession went from one to the other.

Thus Apollo became the great divinity of both parts of the Hellenic world, from the

Opposite, Athena. "Barren, like the briny deep." Below, center, Bacchus, the god of the vine.

Ionians of Delos to the Dorians at Delphi, and pre-eminently the civilizing god of Greece, the destroyer of monsters (Python), the one which, more than any other, demanded physical and moral purity; who, surrounded by the chorus of the Muses and the Graces, charmed the immortals by his songs and the sounds of his lyre, revealed future things to man, and struck the wicked with his golden arrow. "I will love," cries the son of the beautiful Latona, "I will love the pleasing zither and the bent bow, and I will announce Zeus' plans to the mortals."

Under the influence of ideas connected with the worship of Apollo, a greater civilization is born, and a new age of Greek life begins. Society is better organized; urban life expands, and temples are raised to the gods. Songs and music replace savage cries. The gods draw nearer to man and reveal their plans in the oracles, since Jupiter had given Apollo divine inspiration, and sat him on the prophetic throne. The guilty man is no longer condemned to a sure death, and the crime is no longer a hereditary stigma. necessitating the punishment of future generations. Atonement wipes out the sin. It is a world of harmony, light, intelligence, and grace, replacing that of chaos, shadows, power, and terror. Delphi is its center, as it is the center of the universe, and from there the god spreads over the Hellenic people the inspiration for verse, music and the arts, as well as the never-ending revelation of divine thought.

All the Hellenic tribes adopted his worship; and at the foot of his altars, in common prayer and faith, the man of Dorian blood and the Ionian Greek met. Sparta did nothing without consulting his oracle at Delphi, and Athens, along with all Ionia, honored him at Delos by solemn festivities.

A greater fortune awaited the god of Delphi in the last days of Paganism, when the emperor Aurelian calls him the *Deus certus,* and Julian makes him the king of the sky and the world. But even before them,

50

Pindar had already given him some of the characteristics of a Mosaic Jehovah: "God almighty," he said, "you know the end of all and the ways of all thing; you know what makes the leaves blossom in the springtime, and the grains of sand that the waves and impetuous winds roll about in the sea; you see what must be and will be the cause." The idea of monotheism floated vaguely in the midst of polytheistic clouds.

The divinities with the greatest number of worshippers were the twelve gods of Olympus, whose latest theogony controlled the empire and clearly indicated its functions:

Jupiter, the supreme god, obeyed by all the others, the protector of the entire Hellenic race, who, like the Mosaic Jehovah, was also called the very high ;

Juno or Hera, the queen of the sky, whose symbol was the peacock, because its brilliant eyes and spread plumage was a reminder of the stellar firmament;

Neptune, the god of the waters;

Apollo, the sun which lights and the intelligence which inspires;

Minerva, wisdom and science, who gives men prudent thoughts, and teaches women beautiful works and wise resolutions;

Venus, beauty;

Mars, war;

Vulcan, the useful arts;

The chaste Vesta, who presided over domestic virtues;

Ceres, who ripened the harvests;

Diana, "the divine sister of Phoebus," like him, both unmarried and the "friend of rapid arrows."

Mercury, whose original nature is unclear, but who early on must have given men the eloquence for artifice and skill for deceit,

Left, Apollo. "All Hellenic tribes adopted his worship. Athens honored him at Delos by solemn festivals. Below, view of Delos taken from the sacred mountain. Right, the temple at Delphi. "The world of harmony...

Left, Athena (the Acropolis Museum). "The goddess who carried the lance but who had also created the olive tree and taught the arts." Right, the famous Venus de Milo: "Venus, beauty..."

the lie and daring larceny, always honored during barbaric times. Homer had already made him the messenger of the gods; he also led the dead, and perhaps in the double duty, was the personification of the wind which brought the divine words from far away, and carried the poor dried leaves of souls to the subterranean abyss. But why and how did he later become the ithyphallic Hermes, and later divine Reason, the Logos sent to earth by the gods? Different times give the same name to very different things, and the which are one of the conditions of their vitality.

Above all the gods of Hellenic Olympus reigns Destiny, a god without life, without legend, even without form, who on earth has no altar and who, from the depths of the Empyrean where he is inaccessible by prayer, maintains the world's moral equili-brium and subtracts it from the caprices of the other deities. This god who distributes to each person his lot of good and evil had been created, or rather was born from man's troubled conscience, to explain the inexpli-cable and to make understood the incomprehensible, that is, the distant and hidden causes of events and the superior motives which carried them out. Herodotus telling of an injustice that he does not understand, sees in it a divine act, and bows to it.

All the divinities, including Zeus himself, were subject to the law of Destiny.

Thus fatality is at the basis of the beliefs of Greece. And yet this dogma, which is the negation of divine providence and human nature, was to be assuaged: poets and histo-rians tried to justify it by giving decrees the appearance of an atonement.

The Greeks of ancient times did not know a divinity who would later be highly honored in Rome: Fortune, standing on her moving, changing wheel; her Greek name is not found in Homer, but will be found in Pindar, when the progress of anthropomorphism and art will have given a shape to the old formless deity. "O daughter of liberating Zeus," said the Theban poet, "Fortune, you who make rapid ships fly over the waves, who presides over battles and mortal deli-berations, you play with their fragile hopes and carry them to the summit of your wheel, or hurl them to its base."

One of the Minerva's sanctuaries, on Rhodes: "Minerva, wisdom and science..." Below, bust of Dionysus.

6 - The worship of the Dead and domestic religion

Hope for the protection of the spirits or the gods has universally been the origin of religion. The Greeks, like other people, believed that they could appease or seduce their divinities by pious offerings and prayers, by vows and sacrifices; occasionally, in ancient times, by human sacrifices. If the odor of burned victims on the altars was a delicious perfume for the gods, it is because the offering made by the believer of a portion of his goods indicated a humble and repentant heart, the desire to please them with a gift, or the hope of erasing an error by voluntary atonement. It was also these numerous victims offered on the same altar, flattering the god's pride by showing the honors rendered him on earth, which would hopefully guarantee his protection. In addition, he allowed his worshippers, like a good-natured father with his children, to sit at the feast given in his honor and share his victim with them. A sacrifice was a sacred meal, a kind of religious communion among the god, the priests and the believers. These last, to honor the god, ate as much as possible of the holy meat, sacred cakes and wine, served for libations.

The Roman custom of placing divine statues on a bed to offer them a sacred meal, also existed in Greece. A great number of bas-reliefs represent this ceremony, and inscriptions speak of it.

The most complete sacrifice, but also the most rare, was the holocaust, where the victim reserved for the god alone was burned whole; the most solemn, the hecatomb; the most efficient, the one where the most precious blood was shed, like in the immolation of Iphigenia, the virgin daughter of the king of kings. The poor man who had no victims offered little clay images, and this offering was no less well received. Apollo above all exercised a moral action on his faithful believers. A rich Thessalian burns one hundred oxen with gilden horns at Delphi, while a poor citizen of Hermione approaches the altar and throws on it a handful of flour. "Of the two sacrifices," said the Pythia, "the second is far more pleasing to the god."

In ancient days, the temple was either an obscure grotto where mysterious noises were taken for an oracle, or a tree trunk which bore, hidden in its thick foliage, a crude image of the divinity; Pausanias, in the second century of our era, still saw temples of this kind. Those of later times were a great wall enclosing the holy terrain. At the center, built on a solid foundation, was the true sanctuary, the *cella* turned toward the east, containing the image of the god and often those of the divinities or heroes that the principal god admitted to share his dwelling. Near the door, the vase containing the lustral water, kept pure by the addition of salt; under the parvis, or at the base of the steps by which one mounted the temple, the altar, which originally was only a mound of earth or a pile of stones, and later a marble table surrounded by garlands of flowers and decorated with bas-reliefs.

On the walls, citizens' offerings were hung, as well as those from cities and kings, and *ex-votos,* above all from the Asclepiades, in gratitude for a miraculous healing or an unexpected salvation. Often the State and individuals put under the gods' protection, beside the temples, riches, the public treasury or their private fortune.

Included in the precious objects were the relics of heroes; at Olympia, Pelops' shoulder, whose contact cured certain illnesses; at Tegea, Orestes' bones, which gave victory to the Tegeans so long as they knew how to keep them. When they lost them by Lichas' pious fraud, they were still left with Medusa's

(One tried to) "appease or seduce the divinities by pious offerings and prayers": right, a bearer of offerings, from a vase. Below: a family making a sacrifice to two divinities.

hair which, placed on their walls, sufficed to send the enemy army fleeing; Pyrrhus' toe could also work wonders.

The statues of the gods must have possessed at least as many virtues as the relics of heroes. Among them there were very specialized images, including one which cured colds and another which cured gout. The image of Hercules at Eritrea had made a blind man see again; at Trezene, the hero's club fallen to the ground became a magnificent wild olive tree. More often, the images became covered with perspiration, moved their arms, their eyes or their weapons; these were important signs. In these temples, places of popular superstition, everything moved and spoke; there were even periodic miracles: at Andros, the day of Bacchus' festival, water turned to wine.

"The altar of the gods," said Euripides, "is the common refuge." Before him Aeschylus had written in his energetic style: "The altar is more valuable than a rampart; it is an impenetrable armor." Thus the temples, like the churches in the Middle Ages, had the right of asylum. If they were closed to the excommunicate, they touchingly opened for the supplicant. He who brought woolen ribbons or green branches, symbols of misfortune and the invocation addressed to divine protection, always had the right to place them on the altar, near which he himself sat down, under the eye and hand of the god.

Making a holy collection was not unknown. For the reconstruction of the temple at Delphi, a collection was made in Greece, and went as far as Egypt. A number of fines were created for the profit of the gods; they were part of the booty tithe; and among certain peoples these fines went along with that taxing of the fruits of the earth, fattening the treasury in the temples; in the fifth century B.C., that

"The altar of the gods, said Euripides, is the common refuge." Opposite, the beautiful temple of Aegina, the column drums.

of Minerva in Athens received a sixtieth of the allies' tribute, or 10 talents a year. The temples were also rich enough to play banker and make loans of great interest rates. The priests being, in ordinary life, citizens or officials, and pontiffs only on the altars of their gods, the goods remained attached to the temple under a secular administration, and served the State as a resource in cases of public need, rather than becoming the property of a priestly class, which never did exist in Greece.

Greek women, being constantly guarded, could only dispose of their goods with their husbands' approval; an exception seems to have been made for pious donations; and one can be certain that the temples received many.

Certain families, because of legends formed around their names, had hereditary ministries, namely those of the gods and heroes considered as the beginnings of their family, or who had brought the particular worship to their city. But this religious heredity which, in ancient times had created their power, brought them, in the historic period, only honors, and were exempt from no duties as citizens. principal god admitted to share his dwelling. Near the door, the vase containing the lustral water, kept pure by the addition of salt; under the parvis, or at the base of the steps by which one mounted the temple, the altar, which originally was only a mound of earth or a pile of stones, and later a marble table surrounded by garlands of flowers and decorated with bas-reliefs.

Thus, in Athens, the priestess forbade the Spartan king Cleomene to enter the temple of Athena. One of the conditions necessary for practicing a pontificate was the absence of all bodily deformities, a rule which was passed on to the Christian Church.

Another consequence of the absence of a priesthood in Greece was this: there was no more dogma to get in the way of philosophers than there was "temporal power of the Church" to get in the way of the State. The

The sanctuary of Aesculapius' promoted heroes. Before the propylœum is found this inscription: "You who enter this holy circle, be pure, as purity is also chastity."

Crito, not having been placed under the jealous guard of a class interested in keeping it deep in a sanctuary behind bronze doors, Greece became the leading nation of free research in the area of thought.

This clergy, so politically weak, was however armed with a relatively important right: it could exclude a guilty man from common sacrifices, and call for a divine curse on the sacreligious one's head. Standing with his head turned toward the West, the priest damned him by shaking the priestly robe, as if he were sending him from the temple and the city.

Plato created the relationships "of community of domestic gods." These gods were found in the tombs of ancestors and in the home. Thus we must add this family religion to the State's public religion.

Homer considers death as the supreme evil, and it inspires him to have melancholic thoughts: "The generations of men resemble those of the foliage in the forests. The wind hurls the leaves to the ground, and the forest becomes fertile, producing others the following spring. Thus flow the human generations: one comes, the other goes." Even Pindar is struck with sadness, in the midst of his triumphal odes: "What are we?" he writes. "What are we not? The dream of a shadow."

Traditions, come down from the oldest ages, undoubtedly from the heart of Asia, the horror of destruction and dreams in which dear or terrifying apparitions appeared had taught him that the dead began a second existence in the tomb. The tie which, during life connects the spirit to the body, was released, but not broken: the soul, now freer, roamed at night around the places in which it had lived, or it descended to the barren fields covered with asphodel, the plant of the dead. Thus Achilles reigned over the shadows, while his body reposed under the sepulchral mound on the Trojan plain or on the island of Lucaea in the Euxine. Ulysses sees Hercules in Hell, who tells him of his troubles; and he knows that the hero, a past god, lives in Olympus "as the happy husband of the young Hebe." Phryxos' soul, says Pindar, came from Colchis to ask Pelias to bring his remains back to Greece.

This separation of the two halves of the man, this survival of personality after the body is no more than dust, are beliefs that we find at the origin of all religions. Seeing the warrior fall in battle, one moment seething with life, the next immobile and frozen over with the terrifying silence of death, one hesitated to believe that so much energy had suddenly been destroyed forever. But the idea of a second existence was at

"Drink friends, before death turns you into a bit of dust." (Sculpture of a stele).

first very primitive: one gave the dead what he might have been able to use in life: his favorite dogs, his horses, his slaves slaughtered at his tomb. The Gauls and the Indians of the American prairies also followed this custom.

The dead that Homer calls the empty heads, could not expect a very happy destiny from him. Impalpable, their souls wandered silently, with an obscure conscience, obeying instinctive habits more than free will. Minos went on judging, as on his island of Crete; Nestor told of his exploits, and Orion chased the wild animals he had already killed on the mountain; but all missed their terrestrial existence and were terribly bored. The glorious Agamemnon envies this king of Ithaca whom Neptune has chased for ten years in his wrath, and Achilles says to Ulysses: "Do not try to console me about death. I would rather till the land for same poor farmer than be king here among the shadows."

Aeschylus is very much of Homer's mind, also believing that there is another life. When Darius re-enters the tomb that the poet has taken him from, he says to the elderly of Persia: "Whatever troubles befall you on this earth, rejoice each day, because you cannot take your fortune to the land of the dead."

For a long time, the Greeks thought as he did, excepting those who thought that after death nothing remained but ashes. Even in Aeschylus we read: "The dead are capable of neither joy nor sorrow; thus we are fooling ourselves to believe we can do them good or evil." For Euripides: "The dead are insensitive;" and Anacreon sings: "Drink friends, before death turns you to dust."

We must not demand too much logic from the popular imagination; it thrives on contradictions. Parallel to the sad beliefs mentioned here, others, far gayer, existed. Hesiod had the dead brought from the far reaches of the East, to the Fortunate islands, lit not with a sombre shade, but brilliant sun.

The Olympians did not like to meet the glance of one who had just died or was about to become a cadaver. Apollo goes off from

the dying Alcestis, in order not to have to purify himself afterwards; and Artemis leaves Hippolytus who has been abandoned by life, saying to him: "I am not permitted to see the dead."

More charitable than the gods, the people loved the dead, wanting to keep them near them and thus organized a worship which became Greece's second religion.

For a funeral, an obolus was placed in the dead person's mouth, so that he could pay Charon for his passage, the grim ferryman of the Styx, and sometimes one put a honey cake in the deceased hand to calm Cerberus. The body, washed and perfumed, dressed in fine clothes, the head covered with flowers, and put on a processional bed, its feet toward the door, which was open, since the dead was to leave on his long journey. Then the funeral lamentations began, a custom which still

Achilles says to Ulysses: "Do not console me about death. I would rather till some poor farmer's land than reign here among the shadows..." Left: a sarcophagus. Below, funerary steles.

exists among many peoples.

At the entry to the house one put a vase of lustral water, and sprinkled those who left, a custom we have also kept, like so many others of these ancient rites that Christianty either could not or did not want to expunge. The morning of the third day, still on its processional bed, the body was carried by the closest relatives to its tomb; in front marched the flute players, playing sad melodies in the Phrygian style; behind them were the voluntary or hired mourners.

There were two kinds of dead, depending upon whether or not the funeral rites had been carried out. Those who had died in a shipwreck, or whom the victor had left to the dogs and vultures, the criminal, the traitor whose body had been rejected, and all those whose relatives had not given the proper funerary rites, endlessly wandered like the souls in Dante's Purgatory; or irritated and made nasty by misfortune, passed the problems or illnesses on to the families, rendered their lands barren and terrified the living, filling the night with sinister cries and threatening apparitions.

Right, the plain of Marathon. Below, a decapitated statue.

7 - Oracles, Festivals, Mysteries, and Games

In ancient times, when natural phenomena sharply struck men's imaginations, the art of reading the entrails of victims and of interpreting dreams, the flight of birds and flashes of lightening, were all part of religion and politics: thus Tiresias and Calchas were in great standing with the Kings. Then with the progress of lay wisdom, more attention was given to the affairs of the earth than the sky.

Plato said, "God gave man divination to make up for his lack of intelligence." It was as well not the most cultivated mind which received the privilege of lifting the veil from the future. The blind man and the madman became infallible prophets for the mob. Fountains whose waters disturbed the harmony of the human body or the spirit, and grottoes from which gas escaped, producing delirium and hallucinations, were considered places where the divinity was constantly present.

The fountain of Castalia, falling limpid and pure from the Phaedrial rocks was holy water, where all who came to consult the oracle were purified.

"Plato said: "God gave divination to man to make up for his limited intelligence."— The fresco below shows youths consulting an oracle. Right, the Sacred Way at Delphis and, in this city, where the Sibyl's tripod was found, the orifice from which came the emanations.

If we exclude the prophetic oaks of Dodona in Epirus, whose priestesses read the noises in the winds of storms, there ware no oracles in Greece more famous than the cave of Trophonios in Boeotia, and the Delphic temple in Phocis; both were created from a similar source, gaseous fumes read by a priestess or consultant. Plutarch and above all Pausanias have passed on to us the reports of strange scenes whose theatre was the sanctuar of Trophonios.

The mounth of the abyss, recalling the one where Apollo killed the Python, was found in a grotto which was less than three yards high and two yards wide. After long preparations and a rigorous examination, one descend-

"The fountain of Castalia (photo below) was the holy water with which all who came to consult the oracle had to purify themselves.

ed into the grotto at night, with the aid of a ladder. At a certain depth, there was only an extremely narrow opening into which one slipped one's feet; one was then rushed with extreme speed to the botton of the pit, bordering on a great abyss. Overcome by dizziness by the rapid movement, fear and the effect of the gas, one heard terrifying sounds, confused moans and voices which, in the midst of the noises answered questions; or one saw strange apparitions, gleams of light among the shadows, and images which were also regarded as answers. With one's imagination overcome by these illusions one was dragged up, feet first, with the same force and speed as in the descent.

Apollo was less dreadful. For this god of light, interpreter of the will of Zeus, master of men and immortals, everything happened during the day. The authority of his oracles spread beyond the boundaries of the Hellenic world, as far as Lydia, and among the Etruscans, and to Rome, where the books of the Apollonian Cumaean Sibyl were so highly regarded. Cicero called it the earth's oracle, and Delphi was really the center of Hellenic religion, by the concourse of pilgrims and the importance of consultations requested of the god who seemed to be present at this spot more than at any other sanctuary.

In order that the divine deed seem more evident, Apollos answers were originally repeated by a simple and unlearned young girl, almost always troubled by one of the nervous disorders which seem common in certain parts of Greece, and later on by a woman at least fifty years old; finally, Pythia was not sufficient to pronounce to the great number of pilgrims, and three of them were established. These unfortunate women were dragged, drooping and bewildered, to an opening in the earth from which certain vapors escaped. There, seated on a tripod, forcefully, held there by priests, they received the prophetic exhalations. Their faces paled, their limbs shook with convulsive movements.

The Delphic Sibyl on her tripod.

At first they uttered only whimpering complaints and groans; soon, with gleaming eyes and foaming mouth, their hair on end with fright, they were heard to speak, amidst cries of pain, broken incoherent words, recorded with care and painstakingly put into verse by a priest, himself taken in by his faith in the oracle, who had to discover the revelation of the future as hidden in these words by the god. Thanks to the great number of pilgrims, the priests could keep themselves up to date on all that was happening in the States, and among individuals. What they learned in this way enabled them to give a meaning to these inarticulate sounds which fear or hope made acceptable, and which were often made to come true by faith.

69

The Greeks loved oracles. A curious and impatient people, they wanted to know everything, even the future. Enigma pleased them, and called their subtle spirit into play; but they also loved the pomp and magnificence of festivals, so brilliant under their beautiful sky, and they marked with religious solemnities the great stages of their national existence, as they did the phenomena of natural and moral life, which appeared to them as a favor, counsel or threat from the gods.

In addition to the religious reason, Plato found a special motive for these solemnities: "The gods," he said, "touched with compassion for mankind, condemned by nature to work, have arranged periods of rest for them in the regular series of festivals instituted in their honor." The Greeks were so in agreement with this reasoning that they increased these rest intervals to a point where they almost equaled the work periods. In Athens, there were more than eighty days of the year taken up by festivals and spectacles.

These spectacles and games were not the useless diversion of a lazy crowd like the plebs of Rome under the Caesars; they were part of religion and a national worship; they were the great school of patriotism and art, and even morality; "The Muses", said Plato, "and Apollo, their leader, preside over them and celebrate with us." The criminal was banished, but the poor man, even the slave, attended. At the great Dionysia in Athens, prisoners' chains were removed so that they too could celebrate the the joyous festival of the god who chases consuming sadness and renders the spirit as free as the tongue. As long as it lasted. no slave had a master, nor the captive a guardian. In Crete on Hermes' days, it was the masters who served their slaves at table.

Each city had its own festivals and reserved a certain number of places for these soleminities for the inhabitants of an allied city, colony or metropolis. As soon as the service to the god began, the city's business stopped; courts were closed; payments were

Decoration on a vase: Amazons and Griffons.

postponed as were criminal executions, even in Sparta.

As in the Middle Ages in the west, organizations, professions, even ages and sexes had their patrons and their festivals. Thus in Athens, there were occasions for sailors, blacksmiths and undoubtedly many others; in Sparta, it was nurses; in other places, slaves. There were for youths, young girls, married women, special patrons among the gods, and families had their saints, which did not prevent them from carrying out, on the altars of common gods, the ordinary rites for births, marriages and deaths.

"Formerly," said Plutarch, "the festival of Dionysus had a simplicity which did not exclude joy: at the head of the procession there was a pitcher full of wine crowned with vine branches; behind there was a he-goat and assistants holding a basket of figs; lastly, another assistant carried the *phallos,* symbol of fertility." Dionysus presided over the works of the fields, which in a country not rich in wheat, was above all the work of wine–growing. He was also, pre–eminently, the god of the grape, and each phase in the growing of the vine or the production of wine had a corresponding Dionysia. The coming grape–gathering was announced by a procession and games. The youths dressed in long, Ionian robes, carried vine plants with their clusters of grapes, and all the other fruits then ripe. And they sang: "Divine branches, from your boughs drip honey, oil and the pure nectar that fills the cup in which we find sleep." The festival ended in foot races; in the wine received in a vase full to overflowing.

There was another festival when the grape was put into the pressing vats. First there were libations and the most sumptuous feast possible; one did not forget to honor the god in consuming great amounts of his gifts; next, a solemn procession. Half-drunk, one mounted chariots which had held the grape harvest, one's head hidden in vine branches, ivy or foliage, one's body covered in animal

Bas-reliefs: a wine-maker. "The approach of the wine pressing times were announced by games. Youths sang: "Divine branches, from your boughs flows the pure nectar which fills the cup in which we find sleep."

73

Joyous festivities, under the patronage of Bacchus.

skins or bizarre garments, then raced through the villages shounting gay comments. Women especially, devoted to the god of fertility, and having their names, Bacchantes or Maenads, formed a separate group, and held in their hands a thyrsus or *phallos*. In certain spots, trestles were set up. The procession stopped here; one of the assistants mounted the trestle to recite a dithyramb celebrating the adventures of the god of wine and joy. Choruses below answered, and Pans, Svlvans and Satyrs danced around them. Silenus on his donkey, jeered and drank. A he-goat, the animal portrait of lasciviousness, was the reward for the one who composed the songs for the festival, which then served as a sacrifice on the aftar of the god.

From these burlesque masquerades, obscene dialogues, pious and drunken songs, grew comedy and tragedy.

The Anthesteries, or festival of flowers, which lasted three days, took place in spring, after the fermentation, when one first opened the vases which held the new wine. A few drops were offered to the gods in libation; for neighbors and slaves, the cup was filled to the brim.

These festivals were those of joy; the Bacchanalia were those of regret and sorrow. They took place at night, at the winter solstice, when the vine was dry and seemingly dead, showing that the god was far away or impotent. Single women, the Maenads or Furies, carried out these wild rites on the slopes of Parnassus and the peak of Taygetus, or in the plains of Macedonia and Thrace. Among the Dorians, these women showed some reserve; but in Boeotia, disheveled and half-naked, they ran along wildly in the gleam of torches and to the crash of cymbals, with savage cries, and violent gestures and delirium. The nervous excitement led to a complete disorder of the senses, ideas, words, and attitudes; obscenity became a pious act. When the Maenads danced wildly in dissolute movements, snakes wrapped around their arms, a dagger or thrysus in hand, which they lashed around them, when drunkenness and the sight of blood carried the furious troop to delirium, it was the god who was acting in them, making them holy priestesses in his worship. And most unfortunate was the fate of any man who surprisedly came upon these mysteries: he, or an animal, was torn to pieces; they ate his quivering flesh and drank his blood.

This lovely design decorates an amphora. "The festival of flowers lasted three days."

"Silenus, on his donkey, made witty remarks and drank." Bust of Silenus in a drunken state.

This orgiastic cult was never very popular in Athens. The great solemnity in this city was, above, all the Panathenaic procession, which lasted four days, in the third year of each Olympiad, from the 25th to the 28th of the hecatombian month (July-August). It was both the festival of Athena and all the tribes of Attica, who, at the foot of her altar, were united into one people; it was also the festival of war and agriculture, and all the qualities of the body and the gifts of intelligence. In horror of the spear-carrying goddess, who had also created the olive tree and taught the arts to man, an armed dance was performed, as well as chariot races and gymnastic wrestling matches, in which the victors' prizes were painted vases full of oil made from the sacred olive trees; equestrian exercices, in which horsemen carried lighted

75

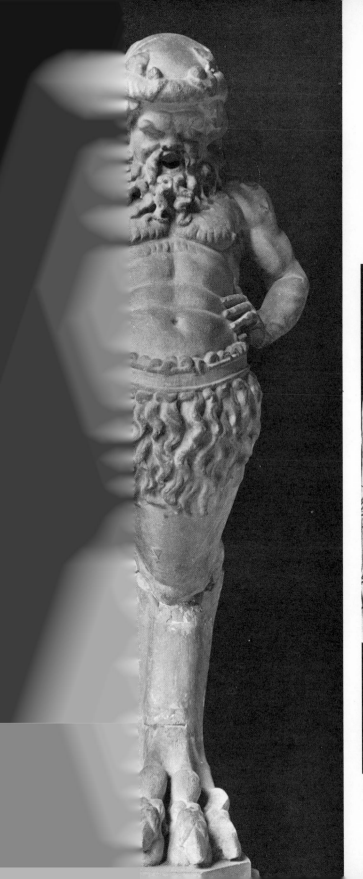

Left:
Satyr holding a vase.
Decoration of a cup. Realistic...
Opposite:
Base of a fountain.
Below:
Another realistic design cleverly placed at
the bottom of a cup: a woman supports her
husband who is sick from drink.

torches to the altar of Eros, symbol of love arousing rapid intelligence; then the recitation of Homer's verses, or another heroic poet, and music contests; lastly, adding a holy and pure feeling to all those which had been born from this solemnity, the citizen who had truly been worthy of his country received a crown before the eyes of a multitude made up from all of Greece. For these grand Panathenaic processions, the time given to the festivals' preparations during which all other work was suspended, even forbidden, was at least fifteen days.

Certain festivals had a long popularity and are still the object of great study; here we wish to speak of the mysteries, above all those of Samothrace and Eleusis, renowned as the oldest and most venerated.

Unfortunately, our information is most incomplete, and we can not follow the order of the ceremonies and mysteries, of which some were considered sacraments. The preliminary purifications, in which all dirt and impurity was removed, recall a baptism, and in drinking of the *cyceon* or holy beverage, the initiate communed with nature and life. Other rites consisted of the adoration of relics and mysterious objects that one held, kissing them, passed from hand to hand, or which were put back into the holy basket, or *Kalathos*. "I have fasted," said the phrase of the mysteries; "I have drunk the *cyceon*; I have taken from the holy chest, and after having tasted, have replaced it in the basket; I have taken the basket and have put it in the holy chest."

There were three degrees of initiation, like three holy orders, since the initiates formed, in the original sense of the word, a clergy. The festivals were under the direction of the Eumolpides, to whom, says the poet, was given the golden key of the mysteries. The 15th of the beodromian month, the head pontiff of Eleusis, the hierophant, always chosen from this family, and which was a life-long appointment, so long as celibacy

*"The great Panathenaics were most solemn."
a procession on the occasion of this festival.*

The frieze of the Parthenon below shows

Procession of women (in the Acropolis Museum). The decoration below recalls a music contest.

was maintained, went to Athens' Poecile, on his head a diadem, and proclaimed the beginning of the solemnity, as well as the obligations of the initiates and those already of the orders; the novices who had been preparing themselves for a long while, received the imitation under the guidance of an Emolpide. Barbarians and murderers, even involuntary ones, were excluded; but any man of Hellenic blood "with pure hands and soul", could be admitted. The following day, the mysteries' members went to the sea for purifications, later repeated on the Eleusian road. The 17th, 18th, and 19th the initiations were led up to by sacrifices, expiatory cere-

monies and prayers, according to a ritual carefully kept secret from outsiders, and by a one-day fast, broken that evening.

The most touching of the ceremonies was the one in which a young boy or girl of pure Athenian blood, and who was called "the hearth child", because he remained the closest to the altar and the sacrificial flame, performed certain expiatory rites in the name of those asked to be admitted to the mysteries. It seemed that these supplications, spoken by innocent lips, would be more pleasant to the ears of the gods: the redemption of all by a child's prayer.

The 20th, the portion of the festival which took place in Athens was finished, and via the holy way, the procession left for Eleusis, carrying the image of Iacchos, given to Ceres' son, and whose name was joyfully shouted by the initiates. The road was only about ten thousand yards long, but many stops were made along the way for sacrifices.

In the evening they arrived at Eleusis, carrying torches, and they stayed there for several days; the crowd gave itself over to various diversions among the solemnities, only the initiates performing religious acts for themselves alone. The herald, before opening the holy gates cried, "Go far from here, the unhallowed, the impious, magicians and murderers". One such, found in the holy sanctuary among the initiates and mystery members, would have been punished by death. The same penalty, in addition to the confiscation of one's estate, was carried out on those who revealed the mysteries.

The temple was on a hillside above Eleusis. A wall, which enclosed an area one hundred and thirty yards long and one hundred yards wide, kept unholy eyes from seeing and approaching the holy place. The initiates wore long, linen robes, and their hair was decorated with golden grasshoppers and myrtle crowns. The most holy rites were performed at night, a propitious time for mysterious things and the drunkenness of the mind born from the over-excited imagination.

"The temple was built above Eleusis..." — A view of the ruins of Eleusis.

One of the most famous was the torch race. The initiates left the holy sanctuary, silently walking two by two, carrying a lighted torch, then entered the outer sanctuary, running in all directions, shaking the torches to throw sparks which would purify souls, exchanging torches from hand to hand signifying the communication and life-giving forces of light and the divine sciences. One by one the torches went out; and from the shadows came mysterious voices and terrifying images.

The mysteries were first meant for the eyes; they were a religious drama much more than a philosophical or moral teaching. But the mind could not remain untouched in the face of these moving ceremonies. Some went no further than legend and stopped at what they had seen; others, few in number, went beyond the feeling to the idea, from imagination to reason, and thanks to the elasticity of the symbol, added, little by little, doctrines which were surely not

"They arrived at Eleusis in the evening, in the light of torches." — Stele decorated with two torches, at Eleusis.

there originally, or if they were, were most confused. Still later these ideas became clearer and in the mysteries there was elaborated a purified polytheism which approached, in some ways, Christian spiritualism.

Diodorus Siculus believed that the initiation made better men.

Man has always transgressed the supreme judge by supposing that he could regulate the order not of the acts of life, but the devotions of the temple, thus considering himself the elect of the gods, having performed certain practices not carried out by others. The Eleusian initiates boldly counted on the eternal blessedness that Homer and Hesiod reserved for a few heroes. "Happy", says the Homeric hymn to Demeter, "blessed are the mortals who have seen these things! He who has not received the initiation will not have, after death, as beautiful a destiny in the kingdom of shadows". And Sophocles said, "They alone will have eternal life." It was believed that even during the celebration of the mysteries, the initiate's soul was in a state of blessed-

These ideas were hardly very old, since the question of the immortality of the soul had always been obscure, and Homer's and Hesiod's conceptions had sufficed the religious needs of the Greek mind until the sixth century. The Hellenic path was then widened by three new forces: philosophers, who were already asking bold questions; dramatic poets whose powerful hand profoundly roused the old world of heroic legends; and lastly the holy brotherhoods which claimed to satisfy the more demanding questions than those of the past.

In addition to the religiously inspired festivals or ceremonies, we must as well acknowledge the importance of the celebrated Greek games: these were collective demonstrations equally important and characteristic of the spirit of these people.

"The gods", said Pindar, "are the friends of the games". Greece had four games in which the entire nation participated: the

Isthmian games near Corinth, in honor of Neptune; the Nemean games in Argolis, which took place every two years; and those of Delphi and Olympia which eclipsed all others.

The *pentathalon,* or five contests, were composed in the following way: there was an undetermined number of contestants for the jump. Those who had covered the required distance were entered in the lists for the javelin. The four top men in this trial then raced, eliminating one of them. Thus there were three left for the discus and the last two for the wrestling match. Horse and chariot races were added, music and poetry contests, and all aroused the same enthusiasm. However, the music contest had only a small number of rather poor instruments available.

Neither gold, nor silver, nor brass was the coveted prize, but a crown of laurel or wild olive leaves were the victor's reward. But in any of the contests it was an honor to win, both for the victor and his city. On his return he was carried in a magnificent chariot; parts of walls were torn down to make way for him; he was exempt from taxes and was given the right to sit in the best place for all spectacles and games; his name was spoken everywhere; poets sang of him; painters and sculptors reproduced his image to decorate public places, avenues or the doors of temples. Fathers were known to die of joy upon embracing their victorious sons.

The Olympic games began at the full moon. Thus, these pleasures could continue on into the Greek night, more luminous than many days in northern climates.

A discobolus.

"*The gods, says Pindar, are friends of the games.*" *Those of Delphi and Olympia eclipsed all others. Races and acrobats. Opposite: the entrance hallway of the Olympia stadium.*

"The Olympic festivals began at the full moon." Left, the site of Olympia. Below, a reconstruction of the city famous in antiquity (by Doerpfeld). A young man ready to drive horses. Wrestlers.

"To the five contests in the pentathalon were added horse and chariot races." Above, left, two drivers. Above, remains of the stadium of Epidaurus. The sculpture below shows a man dying during a race.

Left, site of Karmira, on the island of Rhodes. Asian Greece... Opposite: the ruins at Delos.

8 - Influence of the Asian world on the Greek mind

The civilization of commercial peoples was more rapid than those of agricultural or pastoral peoples, above all if their ships and merchants went as far as civilized countries. As they visited a great many nations, they gathered from everywhere what seemed to them to be the pleasures of a sweeter life. At the same time that they acquired the necessary wealth for encouraging the arts, their minds opened and were excited by the sight of so many things, and their curiosity was more pleased than repelled by these novelties. Indeed the young Greek civilization had much to learn from the Egyptians and Assyrians, these new-born of the western world, and it did in fact take much from them, not only via its merchants, but by its travelers and exiles as well.

Poets and philosophers were born east of the Aegean sea; the first schools of art were founded there, and the first temples were erected. Thus the Greeks received their first initiation from unknown artists of the East. But, like the character in the fairy tale who turned to gold all that he touched, so they transformed everything they received from abroad.

Greek letters, like the Latin and Etruscan alphabets, are characters borrowed by the Phoenecians from Egypt, not only for form, successive order and value, but sometimes as well for the very name, such as *beta* for *beth, theta* for *tet*. But if "the Phoenicians gave the writing, it is the Greeks who wrote."

The oldest metric system that was followed in Hellas, that of Egina, with its division of talents, mines and obolus, is identical to the Babylonian and Phoenecian systems. The word *mina,* a unit in the system, is even of Chaldean origin. Also from there

Cape Sunium: the Attic promontory in the Aegean Sea, facing east.

A fragment of the famous "Tablets" of Mycenae.

to her fiancé, noticed her lover's profile projected in shadow on a wall by the light of a lamp. In order to keep this precious memory, she fixed the fleeting image by immediately drawing its outline; thus drawing was discovered. Aristotle, who did not at all like this kind of story, drew closer to the truth by saying that Eukheir had been the first painter, a relative of Daedalus who, for the mythographers, represented the genius of the invention in an art form. Daedalus was acquainted with Egypt, since his Cretan labyrinth was taken

Athens, the hydraulic clock.

came our duodecimal system, and the use of the celestial sphere and the gnomon, serving to measure the hour by the shadow cast by a solid body on a flat surface. Egypt contributed practical geometry, and Chaldea astronomic observations; but it was Greece which founded science, in creating truly scientific methods.

Of the three sorts of Greek music, one is Lydian, another Phrygian. The flute comes from Phrygia, as did Hyagnis who invented it, and like Marsyas, who, the Greeks said, dared fight with Apollo; Olympos was Mysian. But it was in Greece that music was taught and became a social institution.

Two of the three architectural orders existed on the banks of the Nile and the Euphrates before appearing in Greece. Champollion found triglyphs and Doric columns decorating the tomb of Beni-Hassan, dating several centuries before the use of Doric columns in Greece. Diggers found the Ionic spiral in Sargon's palace at Nineva, dating from the eighth century B.C.

Statues were created and art begun in all of the East; but it was the Greeks who brought beauty into being.

The Greeks, who loved to tell a gracious story as the origin of all things, told that a young girl from Corinth, saying good-bye

"The flute came from Phrygia..."

Egypt, the use of papyrus spread; here writing found a convenient article, and works of prose, which are commited to memory with greater difficulty than sung verses, began to multiply. The first prose-writers came from the colonies.

This activity of the mind, which led the Asian Greeks in the many ways of art and thought, must as well have led them to the great problems of man's nature, God and the world: this research, this study, is called philosophy, and Asia Minor was its birth-place.

Did the Greeks know the dolphin's unusual aptitudes? Below, fragent of a Greek table, decorated with dolphins.

as a copy of the Egyptian labyrinth. The truth is that on the banks of the Nile, as on those of the Tigris and the Euphrates, the temples and tombs were covered with paintings.

The list of Pindar's precursors is long, but barely a few fragments have been left to us.

Terpander, born on Lesbos, the land to which it is said the waves and winds carried Orpheus' head and lyre, and where the nightingales sang their most beautiful songs in the night, added three strings to the lyre, which at first had only four. He had been the winner of the first singing contest established in Sparta around 676, for the Apollonian festivals, and the ancients considered him the founder of the musical art. We have three or four fragments of his poetry, which were religious hymns.

Arion, of Methymnus, was another famous singer. He supposedly invented the dithyramb, or poem in honor of Bacchus, and sang his verses on a zither. Terpander had seduced the Spartans; Arion did even better. Herodotus tells that he was thrown into the sea by pirates, and that a dolphin, drawn near to the ship by the sweetness of his melodies, saved him.

With the ever-growing contact with

93

"The use of papyrus spread... in it writing found a useful instrument."

In Greece, not having had, like Egypt, a priestly class, guarding for itself alone, far from the vulgar non-initiates, religion and science, hidden in mysterious writing, each man could drink from the sacred source, and from this source sprang the free development of the philosophic spirit. Indivisibly united in the East with religion, science was separate in Greece. Like the humanities, like the arts, it found this independence without which civilization would never have broken its leading strings.

Some of the philosophers were called wise-men or sages; they were chiefly concerned with practical morality. Their number, like their names, vary; some say there were seven of them, others say ten. It was a legend by which the Greeks marked the beginnings of moral observation. Thales of Miletus, Bias of Priene, Pittacos of Mytilene and Solon of Athens were the only ones who were generally recognized. Several of their maxims have been preserved, which Plato, in his *Protagoras,* calls "the first fruits of Greek wisdom." "Know thyself;" "Nothing in excess;" "Misfortune follows close-by; but even sadder is he who does not know how to bear misfortune; " "Listen much and speak little;" "What brings wisdom? Experience;" "True freedom is a clear conscience;" and finally the famous precept, "Do not do yourself what displeases you in others." Bias, who put entire store in intelligence, was captured by the enemy upon leaving his home village naked: "I take everything I have with me." The temple of Latone, on Delos, bears these words of Theognis: "The most beautiful is justice."

Perhaps this inscription carved on the door of the temple in Delphi was also one of theirs: "You are," which seems to

echo Genesis, in recognizing only the absolute existence of the Divinity.

The founder of the first Greek school of philosophy, that of Ionia, was Thales of Miletus, born around 640 B.C., of a family originating from Phoenicia. A shrewd observer, he began a great revolution when he learned to replace empiric knowledge by abstract science, that which, by facts, seeks unchanging relations among things. He discovered that the angles at the base of an Isosceles triangle were equal, that three angles of a triangle equal two right angles, and that triangles with three equal angles have proportionately similar sides. This last theorem allowed him to measure the height of the Egyptian pyramids by their projected shadow. His reputation was great enough so that he supposedly announced the eclipse of the sun by which the Lydians and Medes, taken by surprise, were so frightened. He must have also decided

"The founder of the first Greek school of philosophy was Thalesof Miletus." (Also a famous geometer.) His portrait. Below, women celebrating with flowers.

that the sailors of Ionia use as their guide not the Great Bear, too far from the pole, but the polar star called the *Phoenician,* because for a long time the Phoenicians had guided their navigation by it.

We now know that each living being came from another living being, and that life is not a property possessed by matter. But man, and it is to his honor, does not resign himself to be unconscious. On this point, Thales broke with the legendary world; he saw natural forces where Homer and Hesiod saw gods. Some very simple observations on humidity, and the general belief in the flow of the waters around the earth, were, according to Aristotle, the elements upon which the head of the Ionian school based his system of the world. Water was for him what it had been in the eastern cosmogonies, or theories of the creation of the world, the basis of all things because, itself without form, it could become all other forms. "Everything comes from it," he said, "and everything returns to it." The Bible shows, before the Creation, the spirit of Jehovah hovering over the waters; Homer creates all beings from it, even the gods, and if Venus Anadyomene was the goddess born of the white foam of the waves, she was as well the powerful generative force rushing from the sea.

But if Thales determined the underlying principle, he did not separate if from creative force. A natural philosopher, he did not dare rise above the material world to discover God. He thought that the universe was a living organism, and the gods were the very forces of nature, the causes produced by phenomena. "All is full of god," he said.

Heraclitus of Ephesus, who lived around 500 B.C., chose another primordial agent, fire, and denied the existence of an ultrasensitive being; but he conceived the remarkable idea of the constancy of general laws, despite the infinite variety of forms: "All is moving, nothing stands still." Varia-

tions of matter were for him but temporary changes, a perpetual *becoming,* as Hegel would say, an endless flow of changing forms. The philosopher refused, it is said, to give laws to his country, which made him seem like a solitary misanthrope, and grieved the stubborn thinker who did not want to be disturbed in his deep meditation by the worry of troublesome transitory interests, and the proud genius dared to say. "They beseech statues, as if one talked to stones," and, "Jupiter laughs and the world turns."

However, it was not by their few writers and artists that the Greeks were the initiators of civilization. In being the first to guess that the world is governed by laws, they paved the way for some of our sciences. We still admire Aristotle for his work in *Natural History,* and the *Elements* of Euclid, who was almost his contemporary, still form the basis of our teaching of geometry.

Pythagoras, born in Samos around 570 B.C. or a bit earlier, founded another school which bore his name. It is said that he emigrated to Italy because of his hate for the tyrant Polycrates, and set up in Crotona. It is said that he traveled in the East, at very least in Egypt and Babylonia, and one concluded that it was from there that he brought back his taste for the mathematical sciences which are characteristic of his school.

His theory of number, so strange at first, is not without relation to the doctrines of the Ionian school.

The Pythagorian theory of metempsychosis or transmigration of souls, is one of the most curious imagined to resolve the insoluble question of existence beyond the tomb, dissipating the terror caused by the final destruction of our beings, and giving life a moral sanction. After death, the soul, according to its merits or demerits, passed into another body placed lower or higher on the scale of beings; in this way the living universe was the theatre of perpetual

migrations, which had as its supreme end the absorption of the soul, having achieved the state of perfection, by God. Pythagoras also forbade in an almost absolute manner the bloody sacrifices on the gods' altars, and dissuaded his disciples from the habitual consumption of meat. As he purified the idea of divinity and life, so he purified morality, which is always dependent upon these two, and achieved, at certain points, a height which reminds one of Christianity. He taught not only justice, which for him was the basis of all virtue, but also temperance, chastity and modesty. One could also see at the basis of his thought the principle which became the axiom of modern science: "Everything changes; nothing is destroyed."

We have tried to show, in this rapid sketch, the ardor with which the Greek colonies, especially those of Asia, were led in all the directions in which the human spirit can hope to find beauty and truth. They widened the paths which Greece itself in turn followed and was to further enlarge. Thus the colonies have both Greece's and the world's gratitude, since without them, without their various works, often inexperienced but nearly alway magnificent, the Periclean century, so rich in masterpieces, either would not have been achieved at all, or would have been far below what it was.

Pythagoras. "One could see at the base of his thinking the principle which became the axiom of modern science: everything changes, nothing is destroyed."

9 - Pericles' Athens

Pericles was born in 494 B.C., four years before the first encounter between Greece and Asia. He had a beautiful body, and nature, as if to show his vast intelligence, had given him an inordinately large head, which is why artists were always careful to portray him wearing a helmet.

He moved not with sudden gestures, but with calm and serenity. Prudence, in its greatest meaning, guided his conduct. For him, all was subject to thought. "Never," said Plutarch, "did he go before the tribunal without first praying to the gods not to allow a useless work to escape his mouth on the subject he was discussing." He had studied physics and philosophy, meditated on government, but above all he studied the Athenians. No one was better acquainted with these people; no one saw their weaknesses more clearly, not in order to take advantage of them, but to struggle to strengthen them.

As soon as he began to concern himself with the affairs of state, he devoted himself to it completely; but in order not to be conspicuous, he rarely acted by himself, most often sending representative agents to appear in public places. Hir hand was felt but he was not seen.

One of his enemies, a base and evil man, followed him for an entire day, swearing at him on the public square, continuing his insults even as he followed him home; Pericles did not even turn around; but once at home, called a servant to conduct the man home by torchlight. He did not indulge in loud plea-

Left, the temple of Zeus, in Athens, and opposite, a general view of the city, from the Acropolis.

99

sures; he refused all invitations to feasts or festivals. He was never seen outside his house, if it was not to go to a council or to the public square. In order not to divert his attention from the affairs of State by his own private fortune, and perhaps as well to make known his frugality, he had, each year and at the same time, all the products of his land sold; and each day he had purchased at the market whatever was needed for the maintenance of his household, which was ruled with economic severity. But he was not a man of sad or savage temperament; for pleasure he received a few friends and relaxed from work, discussing art with Phidias, literature with Euripides and Sophocles, and philosophy with Protagoras, Anaxagoras or Socrates. The Milesian Aspasia, the link in this group of extraordinary minds, added to her questions an inimitable grace which, even more than her beauty, charmed Socrates and had seduced Pericles.

The people had at last found a leader they could admire and not fear. They also had unlimited confidence in him. Never had any man had such power in Athens. Without any special title, without specific authority, "and only by the authority of his genius and virtues", Pericles was master, more nobly than Augustus of Rome, master of Athens for fifteen years.

One must represent the Athenians of this time not like the plebs of Rome, whose only care was bread and games, but as an aristocracy elevated by its tastes, its elegance, its intellectual cultivation and its custom of authority, above the ordinary position of other peoples. The populace in Athens, included slaves, foreigners, metics, this crowd of more than one hundred thousand souls crowding the city and Piraeus; the aristocracy was fifteen to twenty thousand citizens who alone, judged and legislated, who dispensed with duties and alone fulfilled them, and decided the fate of half of Greece.

Wealth came from trade, industry and banking, which redistributed it among a very large number of citizens; it was in fact so well distributed that Isocrates could say: "There is no one so poor that he must shame the State by begging."

Athens now had a flourishing industry, and its arms, metal-works, furniture and leather excelled all similar products on the market; its pottery went as far as Gades (Cadiz); its art objects, fabrics and books went everywhere. Fish and wine were imported from the islands; purple and glass-ware came from Tyre; Phoenician ship-owners went far to search for tin; papyrus came from Egypt; gold, iron, wool and fabrics came from the Asian coast; grains, leathers, tar, rope, construction wood and numerous slaves came from the lands bordering the Hellespont and the Euxine or Black Sea. Trade, protected on all Greek waters by the

Pericles (left): "Nature had given his head an unusual breadth, thus having artists always carefully represent him with a helmet." Opposite, Aspasia.

Refinements: a perfume-burner, and ear-rings.

"One must represent the Athenians of this time as an aristocracy elevated by its tastes, its elegance..."
Opposite: accessories of two elegant women, from a stele.
Right: a sandal.
Below: sculpture and decoration of a vase. The refinement of the shoe grows out of a very old taste.

Athenian pottery was reputed in the entire Mediterranean basin. "Its drachmas were accepted everywhere; the trade of silver was very active." Right: Greek money.

naval fleet, was so active that Isocrates called Piraeus "the market-place of all Greece". And it was, not only by the merchants customs, but by virtue of treaties and laws as well. Other tradesmen committed themselves to send only certain merchandise to this port, and an Athenian could take a shave on a boat leaving Piraeus only on the condition that the ship would return with cargo.

A writer has left us a description of the habits of the people of Piraeus: "One imagined that he was transported to one of our great maritime cities, since one encounters the same agreements, the same frauds, the same dangers one meets up with here."

Athens had strong currency, in demand everywhere. "In most cities," said Xenophon, "money has a value only locally, and consequently, merchants are forced to exchange their provisions for others. But Athens is different: its drachmas are accepted everywhere." In order to increase the power of credit, counterfeiters were punished by death. Silver trade was also very active. There were investing companies and moneylenders who drew dividends. Bankers made loans on vouchers of precious objects; they had their account books in whey they wrote entries on the receiving or leaving of funds, their correspondence, and if not a bill of exchange, at least the check. Without an official position, the bankers were the trustees of documents and contracts. They made loans to the cities and in a manner underwrote loans to the State. Lastly it must be added that the republic taxed only 2 to 100, ad valorem; that its trade tribunals took care of trials throughout the winter; that the severity of legislation on debts guaranteed the execution of contracts; and finally that the high price of silver which was loaned at times at the rate of 18 to 100, and even higher, enabled capital-holders to rapidly amass a fortune.

Can man grow in the midst of such prosperity? It is not certain...

Aristophanes represents Athens exchanging

the good old-fashioned habits for a ruinous luxury. The two peoples, those of Solon and the contemporaries, are personified by the simple, good-natured Strepsiade, and by his son Phidippide, who is ruining him with horses; the father is merely a machine for paying his son's debts. Awakened at night by the troubles they are causing him, he tosses nervously in bed, suddenly hearing Phidippide in his sleep speak of horses and expenses. "Oh", cries the poor old father, "now what have I lost?" Strepsiade was a good farmer, happy far from the city; but then luxury and civilization began to fascinate him; everyone rushes to it and burns there, like the moth and the flame, "Ah," cries Strepsiade, addressing his sleeping son, "damn the day I married your mother. I was leading a happy life in the fields, common, unpolished, inelegant, surrounded by bees, sheep, olives. Then I took it into my head to marry Megacles' niece, me, a country fellow, and a city woman, pompous, loving luxury, raised at Caesyra's school. When I came close to her, she smelled the wine on me, and the odor of baskets of fruit and piles of wool; she, all perfumed with unguents and saffran, spoke only of expenses, entertainments, feasts. I cannot say that she did nothing, for she did weave cloth, and I showing her this coat said to her, "M'love, you're weaving too tightyly". Then this son comes along. And she takes him tenderly to her breast, saying to him. "When will you be big enough to drive a chariot to the city, like Megacles, wearing a saffron-colored coat?" And I on my side said to him. "When will you be big enough to lead the goats, like your father, dressed in an animal skin?" But he didn't listen to me, and he brought the misery of horses to my fortune."

Pericles wanted all citizens to be guaranteed a subsistence income. The poorest were sent to the many colonies he founded, where they became landowners. For those who stayed in the city, they found sufficient resourses for work in the arsenals and in constructions

The site of the most famous monument in the world.

Sculpted and painted Greek ships. Greece is a land almost entirely surrounded by the sea. "Each day the Athenian sees his ships leave from Piraeus..."

"... They had their account books, and if not the bill of exchange, at least the check... The Republic raised an ad valorem duty of only 2 to 100..."

Many decorations recall the activity of a people who were born traders.

begun by Pericles, in the trade whose center was Athens, in the indemnity of an obolus given to judges and all men of the population who attended the assemblies; lastly, in military service, which brought a considerable pay. Thanks to the gentle climate, the Athenian did not have to worry about his clothing, lodging and food, expenses to which the northerner is condemned. Free distribution of grains, not periodically as in Rome, and sacrifices, at the expense of the State, where as many as three hundred cattle and five hundred goats were burned, took care of the people.

Athens had to be worthy of its people and its empire. In order to embellish it with immortal monuments, Pericles did not hesitate to use money from related treasuries. He said that from the moment these duties were fulfilled, and there was efficient protection, no one could question his actions. The people and the city benefited from this attitude. A mass of workers in all industries found a means of employing their hands and earning a living in legitimate gain; there were professions organized by leaders for quarrying and cutting marble, casting bronze, working gold, ivory, ebony and cedar, used in the construction of public buildings or statues of the gods, for sculpting the rich ornamentation of temples or decorating them with brilliant paintings.

This is Pericles' description of the industrial activities of the Athenians: we must buy stone, brass, ivory, gold, ebony, cypress; and innumerable workers, carpenters, masons, black-smiths, stone cutters, dyers, goldsmiths, embroiderers, turners, cabinet-makers, painters, are busy creating with them. Ship-owners, sailors and pilots bring an immense quantity of the material by sea; carriers and drivers bring them by land; wheelwrights, cord-makers, stone-cutters, harness-makers, pavers, work them; each boss, like a general in the army, has around him a troop of artisans without a specific job,

The reproduction of a grill in sculpted stone: it decorated a store in the trade port of Delos.

a great reserve used subordinately.

Pericles handed the supreme responsibility of these works over to Phidias who, like Alexander, had in turn worthy lieutenants to command. The Parthenon, or Virgin's Temple, entirely of Pentelican marble, also called the *Hecatombedon,* because of the length of its *cella* (100 Greek feet), was the work of Ictinus. Coroebos began the temple of Eleusis, one of the largest in Greece. Callicrates directed the construction of a third wall which cut into two zones the long, wide avenue leading to Athens from the sea, in such a way that if the enemy seized one, the other remained free, permitting communications between the city and the ports.

The Milesian Hippodamos founded Piraeus, the first city in Greece built on a regular plan, and also the first whose commercial prosperity and defense were assured by great and costly works. Inscriptions found at Piraeus show that the maritime arsenal contained places for 372 ships.

The *Odeon,* meant for music contests, was built on the model of Xerxes pavilion, and one rebuilt the Erectheum, the principle work in the Ionic order, as the Parthenon is the masterpiece of the Doric order. The magnificient vestibule of the Acropolis, the Proylaea, all in marble, costing 2,012 talents, more than the Republic's annual revenue, was the work of Mnesicles.

And yet, there was grumbling about the considerable sums of money used for these works. The rich above all complained of a lavishness that was destroying the treasury, and called upon the rights of the allies whose tributes were being used to "gild and embellish the city like a coquettish woman one covers with precious gems, and to erect magnificient statues and build temples, one of which alone cost 1,000 talents". But of course Pericles silenced them with a word. "Athenians", he said one day at a full assembly, "do you find that I am making too many expenditures?" "Yes", was the reply from everywhere. "Well then", he

Peristyle gallery of the Parthenon, and Caryatids of the Erechtheum. Below: the great Phidias worked here (the remains of his workshop, in Olympia).

"*The Erechtheum, masterpiece of the Ionic order (above) as the Parthenon (below) is the masterpiece of the Doric order...*"

Detail of a frieze from the Acropolis. Below, a reconstruction of the Acropolis.
"Thus Athens was Minerva's city, intelligence armed."

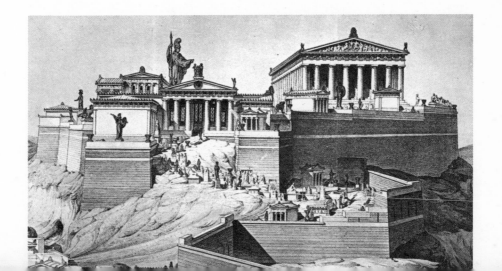

answered, "it shall be I who shall bear them; but also, as is fair, it will be amy name alone which will be carved on all these monuments".

These words must not be taken too seriously, since Pericles would never have been able to place 1,00 talents in the treasury; but the feeling attributed to the people is true. Soon enough a patriotic pride animated this people, proud of its beautiful city. Each citizen, even the most obscure, felt himself important, not seeing any difference between the education of the rich and the poor. He listened to the most clever orators; he discussed a question of art with Phidias and decided the contests of tragedies between Sophocles and Euripides. Every day the Athenian saw his ships leave from Piraeus, some for the Euxine, others for Thrace and Egypt; still others parted for the Adriatic or the coasts of Italy and Sicily. And glancing at the sea around him, his domain, he sees Athens, by its monuments, correspond to the grandeur of the empire. Indeed, Athens was Minerva's city, intelligence armed.

Procession. Opposite, one of innumerable witnesses to the charm of Greek women.

10 - Humanities, Arts and Medicine

Pericles, more than any other chief of State, was as much concerned with the higher interests of the mind as he was about the well-being and power of his people.

Through the events in its history. Athens had acquired the character of a democratic society; it was then necessary, via a broad public education system, to diminish the differences of intellectual cultivation which existed among the citizens, so that moral equality could guarantee political equality. Pericles instituted music contents for the Panathendiacs, these solemn festivals attended by the entire population of Attica, in which runners, athletes and poets came to compete for the crown of honor offered by the Republic, and where a law ordered that the poems of Homer be read to the people, as well as the Perseides of Chaerilos, the slave from Samos, poet of victory and liberty who, it was said, was given by Athens a gold piece for each of his verses. Xenophon said that Pericles increased the city festivals to a point where there were more in Athens than in any other city in Greece, eighty each year; not eighty days of laziness or debauchery, but great national solemnities, during which the pleasures of the mind mingled with the sight of religious pomp, the greatest perfection of art and cheer. Thus painters, orators and poets united to animate glorious and revered memories; and where the theatre, despite satiric drama and comedy, was, in the works of the great tragedians, a moral instruction.

Dramatic presentations were primarily, in Athens as in Rome and Europe of the middle ages, religious festivals. It was believed that the prosperity of the city concerned obliged that the solemnities be celebrated with a magnificence that would please the gods.

117

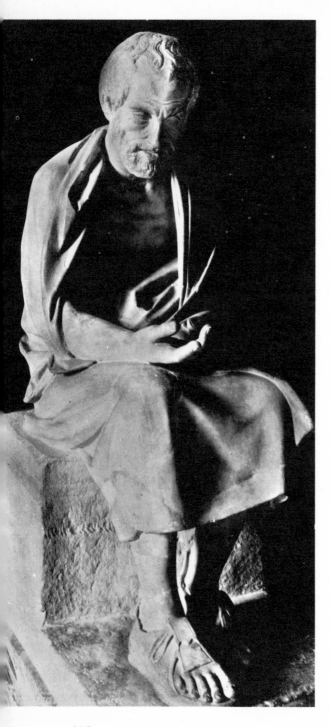

Spectators at the theatre, like the faithful at the altar, felt that they were performing a holy act. The theatre of Bacchus had been constructed in such a way that it could accomodate the entire population. Theatrical presentations were a liturgical institution. This can be seen even in the boldest plays of Aristophanes, where between two obscenities one heard a holy prayer.

Thus in the midst of these glorious demonstrations of thought and art, the place of honor was justly given to dramatic poetry, the most magnificent flowering of the Athenian genius.

The first in time to urge man's spirit toward a superior ideal was Aeschylus, whose dramas have the twin character of powerful works: simplicity and grandeur. The poet was also a valiant soldier, a fine citizen and a believer. His work is moved by both patriotic and religious enthusiasm.

Aeschylus said of his dramas that they were no more than remains of the great Homeric feast: he was right. His tragedies, true epic fragments, have a deep brilliance and mysterious majesty; a formidable Divinity. Destiny, exists throughout them, silent and invisible, followed by Nemesis, divine jealousy, which allows no human grandeur to go beyond a certain fixed limit; both fill the spectator's soul with poignant emotions and superstitious terrors.

Sophocles was almost the same age as Pericles, since his birth is placed around 498, more probably 495; he was also a contemporary of Aeschylus, thirty years older than Euripides, and fifteen years younger than Herodotus, whom he celebrates in a poem. He had be chosen at Salamis, because of his great beauty, to lead the chorus of adolescents who sang, while dancing around the trophy, the victory hymn; he lived until 406, which made him nearly ninety years old at death, just under the number of tragedies he wrote. Thus he saw all the greatness of Athens, as well as the beginning of its decline.

Left, Sophocles: "Ninety years of existence, a bit short of the number of his tragedies."
Above: a tragic scene, and below, Œdipus questioning the Sphinx.

It is said that towards the end of his life, his son Iophon wanted to confine him, saying that he was no longer in complete possession of his faculties. In defense Sophocles read to the judges a description of Attica that he had just written at the age of eighty-nine. Travelers find that it is still precise, but no translation can truly render its harmonious grace; here are several lines: "Stranger, you have come to the most beautiful place on earth, the land of swift horses, where the nightingale sings its melodies among the sacred foliage, sheltered from the sun's fire and winter's cold. Here Bacchus wanders with the nymphs, his divine maidens; and under the heavenly dew forever flourishes the narcissus, the crown of great goddesses, and golden saffron..."

Sophocles, in *Œdipus Rex,* shows love without ever daring to speak of it, and gives women a position that Aeschylus never grants them. Many heroes had been celebrated by the epic muse and on Pindar's

lyre. Opposite the valiant men, Sophocles puts Antigone, equal to them in courage and surpassing them in devotion.

The subject of the *Trachinian Women* is the death and apotheosis of Hercules. This poem would be of little interest without the role of Dejanira, a woman devoted to the hero, and sympathetic to the unhappy situation of the captives, even when she finds a rival among them. She does not loathe young Iole with jealousy, but accuses her of love: "Eros conquers even the gods, as he conquered, me, and so why not another as well? I would be mad to accuse my husband if he is struck with this pain, or this woman who has done me no injustice. For her I have a most profound pity, seeing how her beauty has undone her.".

Euripides, born, according to Aristophanes of an inn-keeper and herb-seller (480 B.C.), had the difficult existence and clouded spirit of the self-made man who does not achieve his wishes: at home, quarrels and repudiation, and never a smile on his sad face; in the theatre, rare applause, sometimes rebels, and of ninety plays presented, only four victories; Aristophanes as an adversary; a horrible death in the jaws of dogs; and as a last iniquity and slander, a poisonous spring running near his tomb in Macedonia. And yet Euripides is a great poet and the most popular of the Greek tragedians.

In the general history of the theatre, two periods can be established: in the first, the mysteries or religious drama; in the second, human drama. Euripides belongs to the second; he initiated modern theatre by bringing to the stage his contemporaries with ancient titles, combining them with eternal passions. A characteristic trait of his tragedy is the position—he gives to womens and to love: it is the heart of all his dramas. His Phaedra,

"A characteristic trait of Euripides' tragedies is the position he gives to women and love." The bas-relief above shows the author (whose bust we see on the right) protected by Bacchus. For him "woman is the most shameless of all animals."

the victim of Aphrodite, is the ancestress of all those stirred, charmed or tortured by Eros. His two wives must have caused him such sadness in life that he got revenge in his theatre, with such bitterness against their sex that he was called the misogynist; and yet several of his heroines have become immortal for their devotion and sacrifices. One excuses Euripides for having written that woman is the most shameless of all animals.

Comedy, which was born with its sister tragedy in the Dionysian festivals, was in the hands of Aristophanes a weapon for combat, striking especially science and philosophy, the bravest generals, the greatest orators and the wisest men. The only thing this comedian did not laugh at was himself.

Listen to this dialogue between Demosthenes and the butcher who, say the oracles, is destined to govern Athens, and whom the conservatives want to put opposite Cleon:

Demosthenes. Are you of respectable birth?

Butcher. By the gods, certainly not! I come from the riffraff.

Demosthenes. A lucky man! How well everything is working out for you.

Butcher. But I have absolutely no education, except that I know the letters of the alphabet fairly well.

Demosthenes. Ah, beware! Knowing the alphabet fairly well could be harmful. The Republic wants neither a wise man nor a respectable man for the government. It needs a dunce and a rogue.

And these replies:

Chremylus. Are you a laborer?

The Sycophant. Do you think I'm mad?

Chremylus. A merchant?

The Sycophant. I use the word when it's convenient.

Chremylus. But don't you have a trade?

The Sycophant. No, by Jupiter.

Chremylus. Then what do you live on, if you do nothing?

The Sycophant. I keep an eye on public and private affairs.

Actors, chorus members and musicians before the representation of a satyric drama, from a painting decorating an amphora. In the center, Dionysus, stretched out on a reclining bed, beside Ariadne, his wife.

The people opposite have given themselves cocks' heads, and follow a flute player.

Comic actors. "Comedy, which was born in the festivals of Dionysus, was, in the hands of Aristophanes, a fighting weapon."

The theatre of Dionysus in Athens. Left, spectators.

Left, the theatre at Delphi, and below, that of Epidaurus. On the photo opposite, taken at the theatre of Delos, we can notice the channels for rain water.

One must add that there were now two groups of people in the city: the old Athenians, among which there survived the remaining aristocracy, too weak to rule, but strong enough to help in maintaining some control, and which the war had gathered in Piraeus. This group, a restless, envious and half-starved mob, wanted to live off enemy booty, extortions from the allies, and the taxes and confiscations of the rich. United in the Agora, these two groups made up a single people, and the second, made up of the poor people of the city, dominated. It was this group which ruled legislated, administered and jugded, and was not demanding about the merits of those they chose for their leaders; from Pericles they went to Cleon, from Cleon to Hyperbolos, from him to Syracosios, and any good talker who knew how to cajole and deceive quickly became an important person.

Aristophanes was too much the son of his century to not be influenced by all this. The atmosphere overcame him; and this extreme conservative, this lover of times past is the boldest of free thinkers at the present time. He calls for the return of the old ways and at the same time works to destroy what is left of them. We have seen such a situation more than once.

Faith in oracles, we know, was still close to the Greek's heart, even in frivolous Athens. Aristophanes mocks and abuses prophets and soothsayers. One of them, the Boeotian Bacis, whose life is lost in the darkness and fog of legends, was very much in favour. His so-called hexameters were collected, and in them one searched for decisions of Destiny, just as the Romans did in the Sibyl's books. Cleon, according to the poet, had made quite a collection of them. While he was sleeping, Nicias stole the oracles from him. But the Paphlagonian had a trunk-full, and the butcher two rooms-full.

Demos. What do they speak of?

Cleon. Of Athens, Pylos, you, me, everything.

Demos (to the Butcher). And yours?

Butcher. Athens, lentils, Lacedaemonians, fresh mackerel, you, me.

Demos. Well! Read them to me, especially the one I like so much where it says that I will be an eagle soaring among clouds.

There then follows a grotesque parody of rejoinders "which the august Delphic oracles made to reverberate in Apollo's sanctuary".

Thanks to the mysteries, doctrines were spread far and wide, sending virtuous souls winging toward the regions of light and the places of gods, to become, along with the others, incorruptible and imperishable beings: the poet's mockery. Falling stars are rich men leaving a banquet, a lantern in hand; since there are celebrations on high, the same can be found on earth, in houses of easy pleasures.

Plato, an enemy of democracy, naturally does all he can to strike back at the writer who so villainously attacked him. In the *Symposium*, he places him next to Socrates. This surprising eulogy is Plato's: "The Graces, looking for an indestructible sanctuary, found Aristophane's soul."

The Greeks did not succeed on the first try to produce the architectural pefection we admire on the Acropolis. As a first dwelling place they gave the gods mountain-tops and deep forests; but they wanted them to be nearer, and from the oldest times began constructing rustic, simple abodes, which little by little were embellished and attracted other arts.

They were unfamiliar with the pointed arch and the dome. One believed to have found them in Tiryns and Mycenae, but if bays and galleries end in pointed forms, it is simply because the foundations gradually drew together and met by touching at the top. This method is simple and barbaric; it was replaced by the flat-moulding and the pediment.

All Greek temples are similar in the general construction plan; and yet the architectonic combinations are numerous, considering the

128

"The Parthenon, built entirely of Pentelican marble, is not the largest of Greek temples, but its execution is the most perfect, thus making it the masterpiece of art."

nature of the different materials used and the ornamentation that decorates them, by the number of columns and the width of the intercolumniations, determining the building's proportions, above all the special nature of each of the three orders, Doric, Ionic and Corinthian. A single element of construction, the column with the part of the entablature it supports, determines this special character.

The Parthenon, built entirely of Pentelican marble, is not the largest of Greek temples, but its execution is the most perfect, and as such was the masterpiece of Hellenic art.

The interior of the Parthenon was made up of two chambers: the smaller one behind, called the *opisthodome,* contained the public treasury; the larger, or *cella,* held the statue of the goddess born without mother, but from the thoughts of the head of the gods, and was like the soul, whose material shell was the Parthenon. Figures in round-relief, approximate twice life-size, decorated the two pediments of the temple. The frieze which ran around the *opisthodome* and the *cella* thirteen yards above their floor, was more than 160 yards long, and represented the great Panathenaic processions.

The monument was finished in 435. It was neither the centuries nor barbarians who mutilated it. The Parthenon was still nearly intact when in 1687, on the 27th of September, Morosini bombarded the citadel. A projectile setting on fire several casks of powder in the temple, blew up part of it; the Venetian then wanted to remove the statues from the pediment and broke them. Lord Elgin, at the beginning of the 19th century, removed the bas-reliefs of the frieze and the motopes? it was another disaster.

An observation has been made about the Parthenon which proves to what a degree the Greeks had a profound sense of art, and how they know how to correct geometry with taste. In the Parthenon there is not one perfectly flat surface. Thus the beauty of the columns is in part due to a slight swelling

A capital, at Eleusis.

because of his magnificence, Nicias had given the role of Dionysus to a young slave, so perfect in his beauty and so nobly costumed, that upon seeing him, the temple burst into applause. Nicias immediately made him a free man, believing, he said, that it was impious to keep in servitude a man who had been hailed by the Athenians in the figure of a god.

From its first to last day, Greece thought this way. Often in the Odyssey, Ulysses and Telemachus think they have seen a god when they happen to meet a tall and handsome man; and the cold, severe Aristotle

Corinthian art... at Corinth.

towards the middle, which the eye does not perceive as such; and both the colonnades and walls lean slightly towards the center of the building, directed towards an invisible meeting point somewhere in the clouds; and lastly, all horizontal lines are convex. All this with such precision! Just enough so that the eye and light gently flow over the surfaces and the monument has at the same time the grace of art and the solidity of strength.

Herodotus preserved a typically Greek fact for us: after his death, Philip of Crotona was revered as a hero in a small public building constructed for him, having been the handsomest man of his time, and the historian agrees with the Aegisthians who created this special god. Nor does he question if Xerxes had truly royal qualities: "In his entire army", said Herodotus, "no one was more worthy of sovereign power by his beauty than he". In one of the choruses in which he was often the prize-winner

A column from the temple of Zeus in Athens.

says: "If there were born mortals who looked like gods, all men would agree to swear them eternal allegiance."

These memories explain the divine honors bestowed upon Antinous by the most Greek of Roman emperors, but they also show how the worship of beauty, which the Greeks had made into a religion and whose theroy was formulated by Plato, formed the artists of Greece, and to a certain extent its philosophers.

The Greks understood the dance very differently from the way we do, giving it great respect and attention. For them the dance was part of religious ceremonies and military education. "The ancients", said Plato in the seventh book of *Laws,* "have left us a great number of beautiful dances". In Dorian cities they were a necessary part of the worship of Apollo, and the most revered and serious people took part in them.

Plato, in his *Laws,* which is a kind of commentary on the customs and legislation of the Athenians, attaches great importance, even in the moral education of the youth, to the ephebes knowing "the art of choruses", including song and dance. "These divinities who preside over our solemnities", he writes, "give us a feeling for order, precision and harmony; and this feeling which, under their guidance, regulates our movements, teaches us to create, by our songs and dances, a bond which runs among us and unites us". Far from dreading these exercise which at other times serve merely for pleasure, the poet-philosopher regards them as necessary to the good order of cities and souls.

In Sparta and Athens the pyrrhic was a military exercise and patriotic instruction. The ephebes danced it at the great and lesser Panathenaics, imitating all the movements of a battle, to attack, defend or avoid being hit.

At this time, each Greek people does not have as its leader a man like Pericles, of whom, without excessive praise, it may be said was the man of this century we are

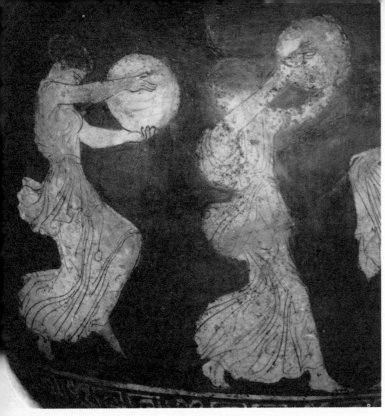

"The Greeks understood the dance differently from us." — "The pyrrhic (below) was a military exercise and a patriotic lesson." It consisted of imitating all the movements of a battle.

now looking at; but those which did not actually contribute to the arts and humanities at least understood them, and by their enthusiasm inspired artists and poets.

Plataea requested of Phidias a colossus of Athena and a statue of Zeus; Lemnos wanted a statue of Minerva, called by antiquity "the beautiful Lemnian"; Delphi wanted a Diana and an Apollo; and Olympia the statue of Jupiter which rendered to the eye the majesty of the master of the gods. Delphi and Corinth instituted painting competitions.

The islands and colonies also supplied their share of great men. Cos gave us one of the most brilliant minds honored in Greece, Hippocrates, who was not only the father of medicine, but a great philosopher as well. From the other end of Greece, below the Euxine, at Sinope, the cynic Diogenes was soon born; at Abdera, on the coast of Thrace, Democritus was still alive, of whom Cicero said, "He was the source at which Epicurus drew to water his little gardens." It is told that, destroyed by long voyages, he was to be known infamously as a wasteful and extravagant man; in his defense he read his *Diacosmos,* a theory on the universe, to the people and his fellow-citizens, mightily impressed, gave him more than he had spent in search of wisdom.

Although the Hellenes had raised Aesculapius to the level of a god, for a long time Greek medicine strongly resembled that of the African witch-doctors. But among the mountebanks' recipes were to be found more intelligent practices in each generation. "Aesculapius' temple", said Strabon, "is always full of sick people; illustrations are hung there which indicate the treatment followed".

Doctors began to study the human body, just as the philosophers studied the universe;

Diogenes, native of Sinope –
and his best friend.

and if anatomical studies could be carried out only on animals, science was none the worse for it. In each important city, a medical service was set up, free for the poor, and doctors found students who paid for their lessons, municipal administrations who subsidized them, and rich patients who often made their fortunes.

Such an example was Apollonides, compatriot and predecessor of Hippocrates, who healed a Persian lord and was thus highly esteemed at the court of Susa, but who was forgotten in an intrigue in the harem and met a terrible end; other examples are Democedes of Crotona and Ctasias of Cnidas, one Darius' doctor, the other that of Artaxerxes—Mnemon.

In the fifth century B.C., two rival schools were celebrated in Greece: that of Cnidas and the other of Cos. It was from the latter that Hippocrates came. His principle claim to honor was that he only wanted to believe well-observed facts. He did not like hypotheses; in his *Aphorisms,* he spoke of the art of healing based on experience, and throughout his life he tried to extract medical laws from the chaos of empiricism. He traveled a great deal, studied man, his surroundings, votive steles left by patients, notes found in the temples and treatments that had been practiced.

In Cos, diverse phases of confirmed illnesses were studied, wanting rather to attack the existing enemy; remedies were decreased rather than multiplied, just as illnesses were simplified by tracing them to a limited number of sources.

His brilliant insights justify the statement made about Hippocrates by a master who had the right to be difficult, considering his own human greatness: "When one speaks of the great Hippocrates, it is not a question

Democritus. "It is from the fountain of this great man, said Cicero, that Epicurus drew his sources to water his little gardens."

134

This bas-relief shows Aesculapius and his family receiving sick people. It is known that the Greeks had raised the old physician to the dignity of a god. (On page 60 we saw the remains of his sanctuary.)

Opposite. Hippocrates. "The Hippocratic Oath is still today the law of the medical profession."

of the man, but of the doctor." (Aristotle).

But this statement is equally valid for the man who wrote: "The doctor will always care for his patients, whatever their fortune may be. When there are strangers or poor people, it is to them that he will go first, helping them not only with his remedies, but with his money as well." *The Hippocratic Oath* is still today, as far as the dignity of the profession is concerned, the law of the medical corps.

11 - Masters of Thought

For a long time spread out over the circumference of the Greek world, in Asia, Thrace and Sicily, philosophers then all came to a central point. Starting with Pericles' century, Athens became their battleground: it was here that theories vied against one another; here began the revolution that started the period of decadence in paganism for the people, and of moral transformation for superior men. The spirit was removed from the ancient religion in two ways. The mysteries, especially those of Eleusis, had little by little released, united and developed the spiritual elements contained in the old worships, and without breaking from polytheism, they put forth the idea of a single god. Stronger and freer, the philosophers, via reason alone, retraced the steps to an initial creator. But in stirring up the great problems that religion had supposedly solved, these men naturally caused insubordination and revolt against it.

While they thus undermined the national religion by reason, the comic poets killed it by mockery, and their influence rapidly spread among a people where everyone read even when traveling. What must the effect on the crowds have been, united there in the theatre in Athens, watching *Plutus, The Birds* and *The Frogs,* of Aristophanes, who treated the gods so irreverently?

Art did its share in this distructive work. Parodies of the gods were depicted on painted vases, samples of which were found everywhere, filling the role of our newspapers and caricatures, while popularizing the irreverent Olympic scenes that the comic poets had brought to the stage.

A certain number of these still exist in collections. One of them, in the Vatican, shows Jupiter at Amphitryon's door, hidden by a bearded mask, and holding a ladder which would enable him to reach, like some common libertine in an amorous adventure, the window where Alcmena awaits him. Near him, Mercury, disguised as a big-bellied slave, is going to help the lovers escape by lighting the way with a lantern. Another vase, in the British Museum, shows Bacchus who has gotten Vulcan intoxicated in order to take him, despite his protests, to Olympia, where he has had problems. On another vase it is Neptune, Hercules and Mercury who are fishing to supply food for the gods' feast.

Aristophanes attacked sophistry with a

"The parodies of the gods were depicted on painted vases..." Here we see Zeus visiting a beautiful woman, passing by her window.

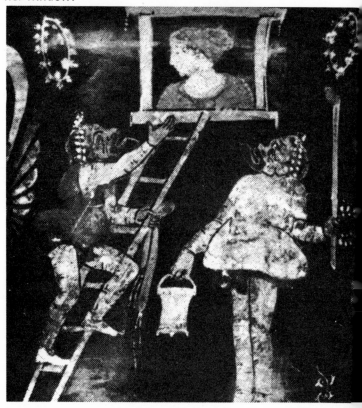

unique energy, without proposing another solution except going backwards three generations. But didn't he himself have all the vices of the times? The true solution was not an unawareness of past times; it was to be found rather in the powerful science just begun by a certain man, and this man was the one whom the poet had most cruelly attacked.

Socrates was born in 469, of a midwife named Phenarete, and a sculptor named Sophronisces. He was quite ugly, which helped him learn quite soon that only moral ugliness is repulsive. It is said that he first exercised his father's profession.

His speculative studies did not prevent him from the duties of a citizen as obliged by the law; he fought courageously at Potidaea, Amphipolis and Delion; at Potidaea he saved the wounded Alcibiades; at Delion he was one of the remaining few who were not captured. The generals said that if every one had fulfilled their duties as he did, the battle would not have been lost. Indifferent to what most men considered necessities, he applied himself to having no needs, and in order to be freer, lived on little, walked barefooted summer and winter, wearing only a shabby coat; and the anger of powerful men, and the hate or applause of the crowds had no more effect on his soul than the heat or cold on his body. Alcibiades offered him land, Charmides offered him slaves, the king of Macedonia offered him his favor: he wanted none of it.

Then what did this good man and courageous citizen do to attract so much ill-will on the part of his contemporaries, and so much admiration from posterity?

This is it. Socrates had imposed upon himself the duty of extricating the moral meaning around which the sophists had created a layer of thick, confusing clouds. Everything staggered at the touch of their debilitating and destructive doctrines. In man, the sophists only recognized that which is the individual; Socrates searched for human

Remains of Apollo's temple, at Delphi. On the pediment was found this maxim: "Know thyself."

nature. He had read on the pediment of the temple at Delphi: "Know thyself"; for him this was the most important science.

In revealing a justice beyond special laws of each state, Socrates showed that this is an ideal that all societies must try to approach; yet he remained respectful of the established order; he honored the sanctity of the family, and found for the mother and wife words that recalled the good woman in the Scriptures.

Indifferent to all external matters, as no other Greek had ever been, to the point of having willingly left Athens only once or twice, he concerned himself with man's interior life, and spent his days looking withing himself and others. The purpose of his life was to convert a few souls to virtue and truth. Armed with two powerful weapons, that of a clear and sharp intelligence which quickly discovered error, and a both subtle and strong logic which irretrievably bound the adversary, he charged himself with the duty of pursuing falsehood. And he fulfilled this mission for forty years, with the faith of an apostle and the pleasure of an artist, delighting in his victories over presumption or ignorance. Didn't he even one day make Theodotus, the beautiful courtesan, know that there were means available to her to render her profession more lucrative?

This teaching at all times and with all people was neither theoretical nor preparatory; it went on from day to day, in any place and any time a falsehood became evident. Constantly among the public, not to take part in the affairs of State, doing so only when law obliged him to do so, he was on the lookout to stop any false doctrine, seizing it and revealing what it hid, its emptiness. He was always seen walking in the city, this man disfavored by nature with his flat nose, thick lips, short, thick neck, a protruding belly like Silenus, round, bulging eyes, though these were lit by his genius. He roamed here and there, sometimes distracted, absorbed in deep meditations, staying in the same spot for twenty-four hours at a time, it was said; often approaching a passer-by, or entering a shop to discuss with the artisan the subject that seemed suitable to him. He was forever carrying on dialogues. From a simple fact, immediately agreed to by the others, he made them draw unexpected consequences, and insurmountably led them, without seeming to intervene himself, to ideas in which they had no doubt. His method became famous in antiquity under the name of *Socratic irony*; it taught one to think and to assure oneself that he was thinking correctly. He also called himself, in memory of his mother's profession, the midwife of the mind, leading the artisan, like himself, to develop more elevated and rational ideas on art, politics, the affairs of State, sophistry, and the questions he himself raised. A bit of jesting was always part of his conversations. Socrates interested himself only in the man in search of truth, a seeker,

as he said; at first he pretended to have great faith in his adversary's knowledge, seeming to want to learn from him; little by little the roles changed, and most often he reduced him to foolishness or silence.

How could this lawful and true man be condemned to the tortures reserved for traitors and murderers? There were three principal accusations: Socrates did not recognize the Republic's gods; he introduced new divinities, and he corrupted the youth.

No matter how much in fact, when speaking of the sovereign power, he said either God, or the gods, or the Divinity, even sincerely admitting to inferior gods, the mind of the crowd, popular instinct, was not wrong: in his system there was no place for vulgar theology, for these weaknesses, struggles and vices of the masters of Olympus, justifying the weaknesses and vices of their worshippers.

And what was thought of these words: "How could the gods be more concerned with our offerings than our souls? If this were so, the guiltiest man could have himself pardoned. But no, the only good men are those who in word and deed fulfill their duties to gods and man."

It was the denial of the national religion.

The tanner Anytos, a man influential by his fortune, and zealous partisan of the democracy who not long ago had been punished, was the principal accuser. Socrates had offended him by convincing his son not to carry on his father's business. A bad poet, Meletos, and the rhetorician Lycon, stood behind Anytos in the matter. The tribunal was that of the *heliastes*: five hundred fifty-nine members were present. Lysias, the greatest orator of the times, offered to plead for Socrates; he did not want this, and defended himself, with the dignity of a man who had no desire to bargain for his life nor to argue the facts of his past seventy years with his accusers. To the accusation of not believing in the gods revered by the Republic, and of introducing new divinities, the wise man said that he had never stopped believing in the country's gods or offering sacrifices to them in his home or on public altars; that he had often been heard to advise his friends to consult the soothsayers and

Socrates. "He was quite ugly, which early on taught him to understand that only moral ugliness is repulsive." "He lived on very little, walked barefoot summer and winter, wearing a shabby coat." — "He was seen walking in the city..." (Below, the tiles of the path that crossed the Agora in the direction of the Parthenon.) "He was constantly in dialogue."

oracles. But when he spoke of his *spirit,* an uproar of mumbling was heard in the assembly. One could admit to some vague intervention of spirits in the the affairs of this world: it was tradition. But one was utterly revolted by the thought that a man had at his service an unconstrained devil guiding him in the deeds of his life.

It remained to decree the penalty; Meletos proposed death; Socrates said: "Athenians, for having given myself completely to the service of my country, endlessly working to make my fellow-citizens virtuous, thus having neglected domestic affairs, functions and other dignities, I condemn myself to be fed in the Prytaneum for the rest of my days at the Republic's expense.". But the death penalty was voted.

His last words to the judges, according to Plato's *Apology,* shows a serenity that Cato of Utica, before killing himself, searched for in the *Phaedo*: "One of two things is possible", he said. "Either death is utter annihilation, or it is the passing of the soul to another place. If everything is destroyed, death will be a night without dreams or consciousness of ourselves; eternal, joyful night. If it is a change in our dwelling place, what delight to meet those we have known and to talk with the wise men. But it is time for us to part, I to die, you to live. Which of us has the better fate: it is a secret for everyone, except God."

He lived thirty days in prison, awaiting the return of the procession sent to Delos, since during the time of this pilgrimage, the laws forbid any execution. He spent his time setting Aesop's fables into rhyme, and above all, discussing the most philosophic problems, of the immortality of the soul of a future life, better than this one, with his friends.

Finally his last day arrived. Socrated devoted it entirely to the talk Plato has recorded for us in the *Phaedo*. At sunset he was brought the hemlock; he drank it, steady and serene, in the midst of his friends in tears; the jailer himself wept. When

"*Socrates lived in prison for 30 days... He dedicated the last one to the speech Plato has preserved for us. At sunset, he was brought the hemlock...*"

Socrates' tomb, at the foot of the mountain of the Muses.

death's cold had invaded his legs and began to reach the upper parts of his body, Socrates said, with a half-smile which betrayed his scepticism without showing disdain: "Crito, we owe a cock to Aesclapios; don't forget to pay this debt". He meant that this death would deliver him from the pains of life, and that he had to thank the healing god. A few moments later a slight movement of his body announced that his soul had left him (May or June, 399 B.C.).

Socrates disciples, terrified by the blow struck at their master by religious intolerance, fled to Megara and other cities. With them they carried his doctrines which spread to all the countries inhabited by the Greek people, and went as far as penetrating the limited intelligence of the Boeotians. Varied as the man himself whose study is their common point of departure, these doctrines gave birth to a number of systems of thought. All schools and movements of philosophy come from Socrates; it is the tanner Anytos' condemned man who founded Athens' second empire, that of thought.

Men coming from all over hung on the words of Socrates' disciple; listen to him, he is the Homer of philosophy. And one of the founders of humanity, that is Plato.

After the catastrophe which dispersed Socrates' disciples, he traveled over Greece, to Sicily, Cyrenaica, and Egypt, studying all schools, questioning wise men, or those who thought they were, even the Egyptian priests, who told him of the great wreck of the Atlantic continent, and with great pride spoke to him of their civilization, fifty times centenarian: "You Greeks, you are merely children." Returning to Athens, in 388 B.C. he opened the famous Academy, where he taught for forty years.

At the end of the *Sophist,* he gives a demonstration of the existence of God that Saint Augustine would have borrowed, in the pure spirit of the Gospel; is it not the Augustinian doctrine of grace "Virtue can not be taught, it is a gift of God."

141

Apollo's temple, in Corinth.

Left: the Peloponnesian plain.

Plato filled the Greek world with his ideas; Aristotle would later reign over the Middle Ages and a portion of modern times. In 359 B.C., the former was seventy years old, but still in full genius; Aristotle was twenty-five and as yet had written nothing. His scientific life thus belongs, following chronology, to the next period; but it is impossible to separate him from Plato, even though they were often in battle.

His *History of Animals,* so admired by Cuvier and still admired today, opens the era of true science, that is, truly experimental research in nature, just as Socrates had searched in man. Until then one had only made guesses, but Aristotle observed, and almost always practiced the principle from which grew modern science: accept only precisely demonstrated truths.

At fifty years old he was at the peak of his genius; for thirteen years he gave two lessons a day: in the morning on the most difficult questions, and in the evening on more common knowledge, from which one concluded that he had a double instruction, secret for the initiates, and public for outsiders, a fact which has, never been proved. Since he walked as he spoke, his students were called by a Greek word which expresses this habit : the Peripatetics.

Of this man, Kant and Hegel said: "Since Aristotle, the science of thought has not gone either forward or backward one step."

He recognized in Nature, which he calls divine, a kind of providential action, and says, in the beautiful passage ending the first book of the *Politics,* that all her works have a single goal, and that never has she made a useless gesture. We can also see in the *Metaphysics* the deep admiration produced in him by the great phenomena of the earth and sky.

Plato: "Virtue is not taught,
it is a gift of God."

12 - The Holy Land of Civilization

Rome began with prose; Greece began with poetry, with poets numbering even among its legislators and philosophers; and all we know of its oldest times are what was sung of heroes and gods. These legendary stories surely are based on an historic setting.

Under the poets' Greece, modern science has discovered a prehistoric Greece. It has studied the remains of a society perhaps as much as ten centuries older than that of Homer, and has tried to find out what influences touched the inhabitants of this land of mountains, peninsulas, islands, with its surrounding seas and skies.

From where did these people come? From Asia, the cradle of the Arian race which, in its long journey to the extremeties of the West, left on the eastern shores of the Aegean sea, in Thrace and in Greece, people whose language and religion had a common base; in this way, cities were built around the great Hellenic lake, capable of understanding and answering each other.

If, in the legendary period, political history is poor in definite events, many are to be found in its social history among the customs which have survived. Thus the family is formed, religion is established, cities are built, the ancient bases of the domestic home, the public prytaneum and the agora, where at first the king's leaders and council sat, and where later the people came to discuss matters and vote.

After the legendary period, traditions suddenly stop; the Muse is silent; the brilliant

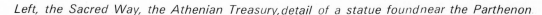

Left, the Sacred Way, the Athenian Treasury, detail of a statue found near the Parthenon.

The Gulf of Corinth. Right: Jupiter, from behind.

light projected by Homer on the heroic age goes out, and we pass through four centuries of darkness. This night over Greece is the passage from legend to history. When established in 776 B.C., the custom of counting the years according to the return of the Olympic festivals also provided the means for fixing dates and chronology. But there are still many gaps before Herodotus' age.

From the 11th to the 7th century B.C., an important fact is established: the dispersion of the Hellenic race to almost all the shores of the Mediterranean.

The Greeks, who liked to hide a profound meaning in beautiful images and tales, told of a sheperd, grazing his flocks on the banks of the sea, who one day saw a beautiful girl come from the waters, smile at him, and call him to her. At first he hesitated, then gave in to her charms and threw himself into the waves. How many enchantresses, sirens, thus played near the beautiful shores, calling the peoples into the blue waves! The Greeks, like the shepherd, gave in, and ran from island to island, meeting at many points along the way, where these three continents approach, people who had the same origin as them, or old trading partners.

In two ways, nature obliged them "to ceaselessly navigate the great abyss": first because of the situation of their country, with the sea visible from nearly everywhere; second, its products. The Greek sun, not suitable for growing grains, despite the protection of Demeter, its venerable goddess, is most suitable for raising grapes and olives, these being industrial and commercial entreprises. A people who has wheat and cattle asks no more of the land which can feed it, and can do without other people;

150

thus the slow meeting of agricultural peoples. But the one which has only wine and oil would die of hunger if it did not exchange products with others. Thus it is forced to live in constant contact with its neighbors, roaming the world with its products bringing back, in addition to other products, new knowledge and ideas. Thus can we be surprised that the Greek people was and still is the trading nation *par excellence,* and that it visited all the lands within its sight, leaving colonies on all these shores?

Commerce thrives on freedom: the Greek colonies were free; those of Rome were dependent because they were an extension of conquest, and because domination means servitude.

While the Greeks passed through the thousands of doors that Nature had opened to them, an internal revolution gradually substituted the kings of the heroic age, the sons of gods, with a nobility who was supposedly still of a divine descent. When these nobles had no more masters above them, they wanted nothing but subjects below them. These subjects in turn, better off and more intelligent than before, believed themselves capable of managing their own affairs; and they then did to the oligarchy what the oligarchy had done to the kings. But they had taken into this battle leaders who seized the government; here by force or surprise, there by, the consent of the people, giving them the power to create order and equality.

These tyrants were also left behind. The abuse and violence led to a new revolution, this time a democratic one.

During this long and painful period of internal transition, intellectual life comes to a halt in the metropolis. But in the Asian colonies, near the great eastern civilizations, the mind is developing. Art and science are born; poetry is added to the Homeric heritage, and the Greek world is lighted by the brilliance of its circumference.

The Athenian domination, assuring the

safety of the seas, rousing industry and commerce, spreading, comfort and intelligence, is Greece's happiest moment, and the most brilliant in the history of humanity. Of course Athens was not alone in Hellas. Word and thought were everywhere; but everything, genius as well as fortune and power, flowed toward it. It was the focal point of the scattered rays, gathering them and sending back a brilliant light to the world. Even before its great splendors, a stranger, a man almost an enemy by birth, Pindar, celebrates "the city of genius; brilliant, immortal, crowned with violets like the Graces and the Muses."

Let us speak our affection for this Republic which had factions and revolutions, but neither civil war nor a revolt of slaves; for the city whose two great enemies, Philip and Alexander, could not hate; for this people whose history opens at Marathon in brilliant triumph, and closes at Chaeronea, with Demosthenes' eloquent outcry: "No, no, Athenians, you have not failed, defending the liberty of Greece to the death." May we not forget this people who so kindly treated slaves, welcomed the stranger, and on certain days, set captives free from their irons so that they too could join the joyous Dionysian festivals. It killed the guilty man but did not torture him; it left the exile his belongings, and even the time to escape before execution for certain murderers.

We love Greece for its poets, philosophers and artists, but also because it was the first in the ancient world whose ideal was political liberty guaranteed by the most complete development of each citizen. The East knew only the calm and sterile unity of great monarchies subject to a single will, almost always the same, despite the diversity of those who commanded sovereign power. Greece was made up of as many independent states as valleys and promontories given to it by Nature for its defense; and in almost all these communities, the inhabitants accepted the religion and constitutional law

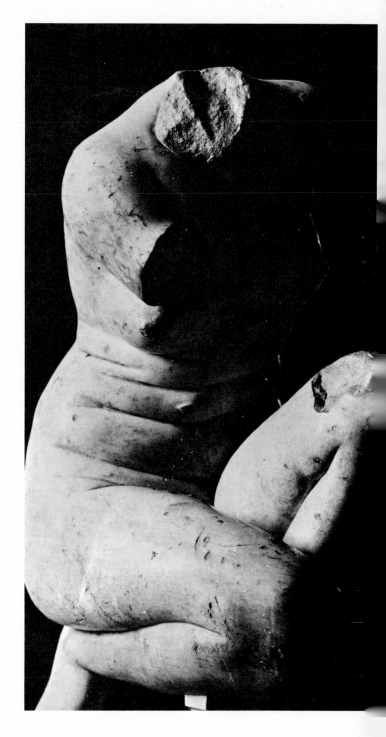

in exchange for a single freedom, that of decreeing themselves this law which governed them.

An unexpected quality found in these cities was charity. The time of institutions multiplied by Christianity had not yet come because they were not needed in the social state. Demosthenes bought back captives' freedom, and gave dowries to poor girls, and he was not alone in doing this. He could say, as in his speech *On the Crown*: "You know, Athenians, that I have been affable, human, willing to help in any misfortune"; elsewhere he boasted of never having shirked his philanthropic duties; this word which we imagine to be modern, was in fact in current usage in Athens, more than twenty-three centuries ago. Lysias mentions another citizen who secretly gave dowries to girls, freed prisoners, and buried dead bodies found on the roads, asking no compensation or reward from anyone. And how many others did like him! If the payment given to those who attended the public assembly and religious festivals had political drawbacks, it had at first been given as a means of helping those who needed it. The same was true of the distributions of wheat to the people from time to time, and of the meals celebrated after the great sacrificial burnings, when the gods were satisfied merely by the smoke from the altar. Hippocrates asked doctors to, in turn, ask no payment from those who could not afford it, and many cities gave medical aid to the poor; lastly, Plato wrote: "We must do harm to no man, not even the mean one."

Naturally, between the shepherd, simple worshipper of Pan of Arcadia, and the elegant citizen of Athens, there were great diffe-

Seated, Venus and statue of Poseidon found in Boetia. Following pages, the Acropolis and Acrocorinth.

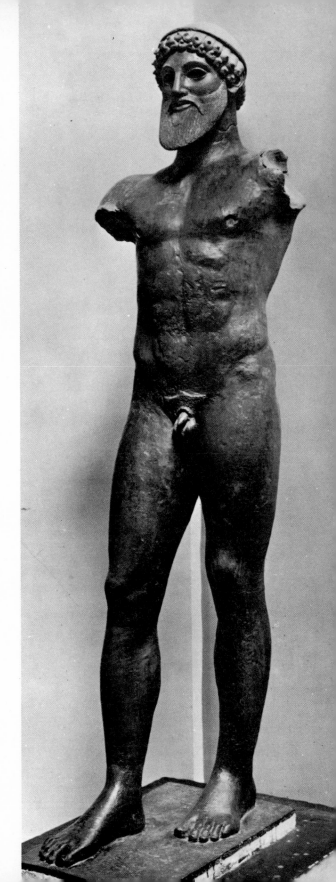

rences; but there were even greater similarities. In addition to the same language and religion, there was a moral communion. The horizon of one is immense, that of the other limited; but both saw the same things, as in contemporary nations: human sacrifice, mutilation, polygamy, the sale of children by their father, as found in Thrace and even Rome, and the servile obeisance of an Asian for his Great King. Both fought naked in the public games, which, say Plato and Herodotus, would have been shameful among nearly all barbarians. Lastly Homer's poems, sung from one end of Hellas to the other, served as holy book for them, creating the idealized nation protected by panhellenic Jupiter.

Thus there is a Greek people distinct from the barbarians, but as well, as Herodotus says, a Hellenic body which indicates the Greek race, later to signify civilization.

The magnificence of the Hellenic life lasted no longer than a century and a half, but this short time was enough to make Greece the holy land of civilization: human thought was born there.

It is not, as an envious Roman said, because Greece produced great and clever writers that it earned an immortal reputation. This small country changed, in the moral order, the poles of the earth. The East had given birth to wise men, but under them the people were no more than docile flocks, ruled by the master's voice. In Greece, for the very first time, humanity became conscious of itself.

Index

Achilles 42, 54, 55.
Acropolis 6, 23, 38, 41, 101, 114.
Aegean (sea) 15, 22, 23, 43, 133.
Aeolian 39.
Aeropagus 23, 24.
Aeschylus 43, 53, 55, 106, 107.
Aesculapius 13, 119.
Aesop 127.
Agamemnon 42, 55.
Agora 24, 114, 133.
Alcestis 9, 56.
Alcibiades 123.
Anacreon 55.
Anaxagoras 90.
Andromache 8-9.
Antigone 108.
Aphrodite 44, 109.
Apollo, 7, 19, 34, 42, 43, 6, 47, 50, 56, 63, 64, 81, 83, 114, 117, 119.
Arcadia 18, 39, 40, 42, 138.
Argonautes 8, 13.
Argos 7.
Aristophanes 26, 38, 106, 108, 109, 114, 122, 123.
Aristotte 20, 25, 28, 31, 82, 86, 116, 121, 130.
Artemis 43, 44, 56.
Aspasia 90.
Astarte 44.
Athena 43, 44, 53, 67, 119.
Athens 8, 22, 23, 31, 37, 38, 42, 44, 46, 53, 64, 65, 67, 72, 84, 89, 90, 95, 96, 99, 100, 101, 104, 105, 107, 109, 114, 117, 122, 123, 127, 130, 137, 138.
Athenian 6, 23, 26, 27, 34, 38, 89, 90, 104, 114, 116, 126, 136, 137.
Attica 6, 14, 22, 23, 25, 27, 39, 70, 105, 107.

Bacchanalia 67.
Bacchus 38, 44, 53, 83, 106, 107, 122.
Bacis 114.
Beotia 39, 42, 62, 67.

157

Depósito legal B. 7904-71   Printer, industria gráfica sa
Tuset, 19 Barcelona   San Vicente dels Horts 1971

Printed in Spain

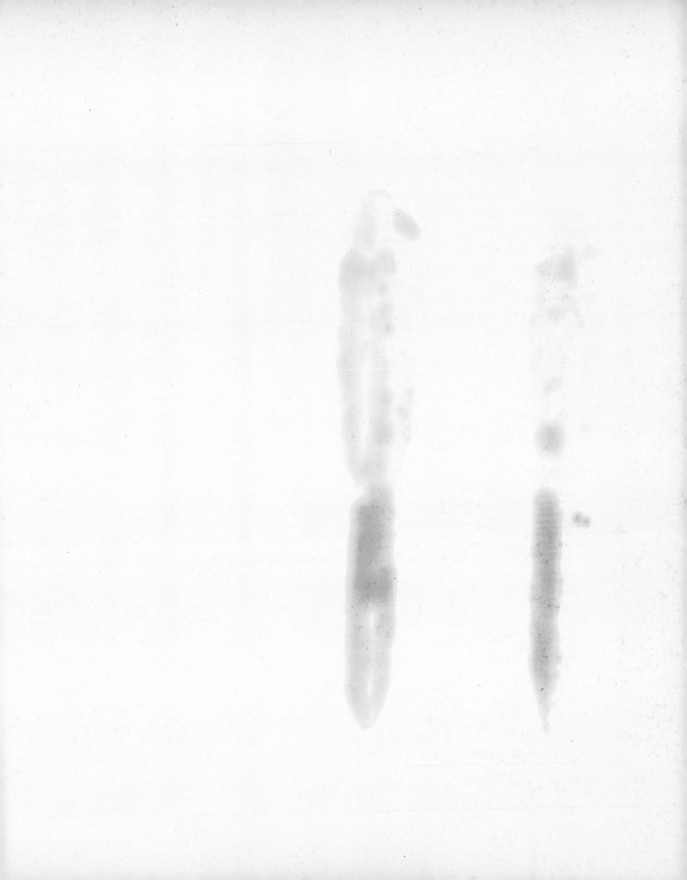